# BULLETINS FROM THE HOME FRONT

# BULLETINS FROM THE HOME FRONT

CAROLYN KENNEDY

*Illustrations by Mark Kennedy*

CHERRY TREE PRESS
Palo Alto, California

Grateful acknowledgment is made to the following newspapers where the material specified was first published:

*The San Jose Mercury News:* "Don't Expect Me to Talk Turkey," November 1982; "The Annual Family Photo," December 1982.

*The San Francisco Chronicle:* "The Mud Bath," September 1985; "Commando Tactics for Kiddie Clutter," September 1988.

*The Monterey Herald Weekend Magazine:* "Plant Mania," February 1986; "A Secret Male Ritual," June 1986.

*The Los Angeles Times:* "Grief Over Gravy," November 1985.

*The Pacific Sun:* "Are Microwaves Moral," September 1985; "The Empty Nest," November 1987.

Meredith Newspapers, the *Cupertino Courier* and the *Saratoga News:* from the period of August 1981 through October 1985, the remaining pieces (with the exception of "Breaking the Thanksgiving Mold") in an ongoing column entitled "A Slice of Life."


ISBN 0-963487-0-0


Ann Flanagan Typography: Design / Typesetting


Published by
Cherry Tree Press
P.O. Box 73
Palo Alto, CA 94301

Printed in the U.S.A.

*For Matthew and Mark*

*Acknowledgments*

I am forever indebted to my sons for providing me with inspiration and writing material, and for their tolerance of being portrayed in print through the eyes of their mother. I am also indebted to my husband, Keith, for similar inspiration and tolerance, and for his ongoing encouragement for all of my writing, and for this book in particular.

Special thanks to Trish Clifford for her friendship and support, both editorial and emotional, as I struggled to get these words out of my computer and into book form, and to Dorothy Wall for her sensitive and invaluable editorial assistance. And last, but never least, thanks to Mike Myslinski and David Hoye, former editors at Meredith Newspapers, who first published my work.

# CONTENTS

# INTRODUCTION

Setting down these stories about my family has been the easiest writing I've ever done. Inspiration always came as my children, by just being themselves, wore me down and taught me important things. All I had to do was get to the typewriter, fast.

Why I turned to writing is a mystery. Until I became a mother I'd had precious little experience, except for grinding out the required college essays and term papers.

Suddenly I was twenty-six years old and trying to hold onto my sanity while running after two lively boys, both under the age of three.

I was in over my head. Little in my life had prepared me for being a Mom. Before motherhood, my primary occupation had been student, where working hard produces tangible rewards—a good grade, a pat on the back, a diploma.

Not so with parenthood, where you never know how you're doing. No one ever tells you you're doing a good job or even an important job. And sometimes the harder you try to be perfect, the worse it gets.

So I did the only thing I could. I started to write.

I started with a journal. One day, when the kids were sleeping, or at least in their rooms, I reached for a pen and scribbled out my feelings onto a calm, non-judgmental sheet of white paper. I felt so much better afterwards, I was drawn to my journal again and again.

I wrote out the strong emotions that children can evoke and which kept me on overload much of the time: love, guilt, anger, more guilt, frustration, feelings of inadequacy, powerlessness, resentment, and unbelievable joy. As I wrote, the turmoil lifted from my heart and shoulders and affixed itself in black and white onto the page, demystifying its hold on me.

As the kids grew, I plodded along in my journal, spinning out my worries and upsets and maybe trying to grow up ahead of them.

Then one day my writing took a surprising detour. It was the day on which I discovered my role as all-knowing Mom had shifted and that I had things to learn from my children.

It was a hot, Saturday afternoon. I'd decided to dig out a large, ugly aralia plant in our front yard. I attacked the eyesore assuming the project would take about fifteen minutes. Two hours later I was still trying to yank the root from the earth, having used every tool in the garage including the shovel, hatchet, hoe, sledgehammer, pickax, hacksaw, and electric drill.

Then Matt, who was ten years old, popped out of the house and offered to help. I decided to "humor" him.

He squatted down, peered into the hole, and ran into the garage and brought out the one tool I hadn't tried—a small hand trowel.

Crouching next to the plant, he dug carefully around the root ball and then stood up. "Now pull," he said. I did and the stem and the stubborn root flew easily out of the ground.

"You just have to get at those little roots," he explained kindly. I looked down and saw little filaments the diameter of dental floss that had been holding the monster root ball firmly in place.

After I put away the tools I went, almost without thinking, to my old college typewriter and typed out the story just as it happened.

Gradually I began writing down more of these little moments. A few years later, I enrolled in journalism classes and then worked as a stringer for our town's weekly newspaper. Tentatively I offered my family stories to the editor, and he used them when he had a hole to fill.

The kids weren't exactly crazy about me plumbing their lives for material and publishing it in the local newspaper. And they always complained that I never told the story right. But they put up with it. Maybe they liked having me occupied at my desk rather than spying on them at school disguised as Room Mother or other PTA official.

The day the editor said I could do a regular column, I rushed home to share my news. I found my son, Mark, operating on a Tom Lehrer tape with his Swiss Army knife, ignoring his open math book.

When I told him I'd be writing a regular column about him and his brother, he replied, "Well if you do, it will be a prime example of the media distorting the facts." Then he waved his knife, asked for the editor's name, and threatened to demand "equal time."

"Don't you know everything is grist for the writer's mill?"

"Don't you mean the common folk are pavement for the media's steamroller?"

I wrote that down and it became the basis for my first official column.

Things went along fine through junior high and some of high school. They didn't read the columns and seemed to forget what I was doing.

Then one gloomy day in winter I came home and was greeted by a very tall, high school person who bellowed, "HOW COULD YOU?"

I soon discovered I'd used a humorous story he'd told me about another high school student, unaware I'd been told in confidence. To make matters even worse, the column had been taped up on the wall at the school office for all to see.

I had crossed a line that day and there was no going back. My sons had grown up and had private lives I could no longer use as grist. I wrote a few more columns after that, but gave each son refusal rights.

Before we knew it, they graduated from high school and moved onto college. The last piece I wrote about them was the "Empty Nest." Usually I had laughed or chuckled as I wrote about them. But with "Empty Nest," I cried.

As I put this book together, our sons have lives away from us. They have their own cars, apartments, and health insurance. I tried to get them involved in the book. Mark provided the illustrations. I offered Matt rebuttal space, but he declined.

We miss them. But there are still lessons to be learned. I'm learning them now. Like when to speak up, and how to speak up, and when to let go.

As I look back on my life with my children, which seems all too short now, I realize the truth of what Candice Bergen wrote in her autobiography, *Knock Wood*. She shares what her husband Louis Malle said about his children: "...they changed my life. The parents are the ones who get everything; children are a gift you give yourself."

So thank you, Matt and Mark, for being such great sons and teachers.

I only hope we've given you both half as good as we've received.

Love,
Mom

P.S. Don't forget to write.

# LIFE
# WITH
# KIDS

# THE FOOD TEST

When our sons were young, they judged every place they went by the refreshments served. YMCA meetings, parties, summer camps, and even visits to grandparents came under close scrutiny, foodwise. Their mouths and stomachs had the final word in deciding whether a place was a success or not.

"How was the Indian Guides meeting?" I'd ask, hoping for some information on projects started, cooperation learned, friendships forged. But they breezed by me on the way to the refrigerator and said things like, "Great. They served brownies. With icing. I had eight. I could have eaten more but some hog gobbled up more than his share." Or, "Terrible. They only had cookies, and the cookies had raisins in them."

And their taste buds had long memories. They complained for years about how when they visited their grandfather, he "burned" the pancakes. But they had a special warm spot in their hearts for their grandmother who let them choose whatever sugary cereal they wanted from the grocery store.

Of all the places they went in those years, summer camp came under the harshest criticism from these miniature galloping gourmets.

After a week of YMCA camp, our younger son jumped off the bus and launched into his critique.

"The fruit salad had shifty eyes," he told us. He swore he needed help pulling his fork out of the meatloaf.

Then he recited the saga of the oatmeal.

"You had to eat your canned peaches fast or else the oatmeal would slither over and get it.

"We watched the oatmeal crawl to the lake. It set a new record. One hour and thirty-two minutes.

"One morning the oatmeal accidentally got into a guy's jeans pocket and when he took them off at night, the jeans walked away.

"We could have made a horror film about that oatmeal," he concluded.

He swore the campers heard the cook chortling to himself in the kitchen each day as he created new tortures for his victims.

As much as we tried, we couldn't wring anything else out of him about camp. "What else happened?" we wailed, thinking of the money we had spent. He shrugged and said, "Nothing much."

One year our older son went to a camp in the Sierra called, "Camp New Horizons." We received the food reviews by mail.

The first letter detailed the symptoms of a disease he had contracted on the first day. Headache, stomachache, fever, chills. He ended with a cheery, "Don't worry about me."

We knew he was back to normal when the second letter arrived.

"It's too healthy here," he penciled. "I am dying from organic (yuck) food. I am sick of wheat pancakes, wheat French toast, wheat soups, and wheat crusts. Even the taco shells are whole wheat."

We scanned the letter for news about the promised leadership training, the wholesome outdoor activities, and learning reverence for the environment, but detected nothing.

He closed his letter with, "Please may I go to 7-Eleven when I get home, and can we go to McDonald's for dinner?

"P.S. Please, no whole wheat anything for at least a week."

There was, however, an unexpected benefit.

He came home two weeks later. He walked in the house, put his sleeping bag and duffel bag upstairs and came into the kitchen. I braced myself for requests for junk food. Instead, he said something I never thought I'd hear.

"Mom," he said. "Do we have any bananas?"

Which goes to show, just when you think it's hopeless with kids, they surprise you.

I never did hear about the leadership training or the outdoor adventures. But I guess you can't expect everything.

# THE JEANS RITUAL

While slumped in a chair outside a dressing room one fall morning, waiting for my back-to-schooler and every so often whimpering, "Hurry up," and "What are you doing in there?" I glanced up and realized I was not alone.

All around me were other mothers, leaning against the walls and clothing racks, wearing the same bored, dead-from-the-eyeballs expression while waiting for their young men to emerge wearing yet another pair of jeans that do not fit.

Then I noticed a scenario that repeated itself each time a fresh victim walked through the dressing room curtains.

Each woman assumes a pinched, worried look, presumably because she knows how much the jeans cost and because she wonders if there really is a pair of jeans in the whole county that will fit her child, and if there is, will she have the stamina to find them?

"Come closer," she beckons wearily to her offspring. Then she pulls at the waist five times, tells him to turn around slowly while she peers intently at certain key areas of his anatomy, and asks questions like, "Can you sit down in them?" and "Do they hurt anywhere?"

In particularly difficult cases, the mother summons a salesperson, always another female, to get a professional opinion. Then the saleswoman will pull at the waist five times and tell the young person to turn around slowly, while she puts on her glasses and eyes key areas of his anatomy. Then she might top it off with a remark like, "Well, it does pull in the rear a little."

By now the young man's face is wearing a distinctly hunted look and it's enough to make any sensitive person, such as myself, vaguely uneasy. I began to understand why my own son was hiding out in the dressing room.

It's bad enough mothers and sons go through this, but the whole disagreeable process seems to perpetuate itself. For across the aisle in the men's department, standing around those dressing rooms were not only mothers, but wives and girlfriends. And these women were waiting for grown men to exit the dressing rooms so they could pick and pull at their clothing and say things like, "No it hangs here," or "It's too tight in the crotch."

Now what woman do you know who would ever stand for men lurking outside of their dressing rooms to pick and pull at their clothing and ask stupid, humiliating questions? It would be grounds for divorce, maybe even justifiable homicide. (Why did you murder your husband, Mrs. Jones? Well, he told me the dress I was trying on pooked out in the rear a little and I don't know, I just kind of flipped out and smacked him with the coat hanger.)

I decided it was time to break this sick cycle plus preserve what precious little is left of my sanity. The next time clothes were needed, I handed my 14-year-old son a charge card, a price limit, and told him to pick out a shirt and a pair of jeans all by himself. To my surprise, he smiled and said, "Whew. It's about time."

The transaction included a phone call in which we debated the fine points such as, "Does cotton shrink?" and "If it's too tight in the rear will it get better or worse after washing." But he came home, the proud bearer of a pair of jeans and a shirt.

We did make a return trip to exchange those size 29 jeans for a size 30, because he'd forgotten to allow room for breathing while he was wearing them. But it's a start.

I hate to brag, but I do feel proud of the revolutionary ground breaking work which I am doing to free future generations of mothers, wives, and girlfriends from hours of dreadful duty outside men's dressing rooms. No, no applause, thank you. Just a simple engraved trophy and maybe a woman of the year award will do.

# THE PRICE OF ORDER

For some people, summer is a time when thoughts turn to picnics, days at the beach, and ice cream cones.

I am not one of those people.

When summer arrives, my thoughts turn toward my children's bedrooms. I see the dusty gum wrappers under the bed, the bowls of ice cream and chocolate sauce remains lining the windowsill, and the marbles and little metal cars that litter the shelves and roll off at odd moments.

On the first day of vacation I bellow, "It is now summer and you will clean out those pig sties before you do anything else. And don't tell me you have homework."

Actually, I have one quasi-neat son and one who doesn't even try.

My older son achieves a certain streamlined look by shoving everything, and I do mean everything, under his bed.

One day the dog crawled out from under his bed with a syrup-sticky plate, a knife, and a fork affixed to her haunches. She clattered around until someone thought to pry the apparatus off. But every time she sat down, she remained stuck in one place.

My other son has never even tried for the neat look. He refuses to admit it's important. He has a unique horizontal filing system: everything falls from his hands directly onto the floor. We call him Mr. Relaxed. He claims none of this matters because he can put his fingers on whatever he's looking for in a matter of seconds.

His father suggests we rent his room to the Marines to practice stepping around land mines.

As August wanes and the room waxes messier than ever, each time he crosses my line of vision I narrow my eyes and growl, "Have you cleaned your room yet, young man?" He slinks away, biting his nails, trying to hold out until school begins and he can plead homework.

Desperate, I utter the ultimate threat. I will "help."

Now in this house, we all know my "helping" is a code word for loud voices, name calling, and slammed doors. This behavior follows certain discoveries, such as he's kept all 365 pages from his Joke-A-Day calendar and they're scattered all over his room. When I am confronted with such things, part of me wants to scream, "What is wrong with you? Are you crazy?" and another part of me says, "Now, he's a person too, and I must respect his idiosyncrasies."

So while these conflicts are raging within me, as I'm trying to make sense out of the clutter, I do what any normal adult would do. I scream and go crazy.

But this year we broke the pattern.

As I grew crankier and crankier about The Room, my quasi-neat son came up with an idea. "Let me do it. Pay me and I'll do it."

As summer drifted toward fall, his idea began to make sense.

And Mr. Relaxed (or "Buster" as I was now beginning to call him) agreed it might make sense too, especially when faced with the prospect of my "helping." The only stipulation was that nothing could be thrown away without his OK.

The entrepreneur and I made a deal. For $13.50 he would enter The Room, organize it, and emerge when the job was finished.

The next day he got up early, ate a big breakfast, dressed, and ordered, "Bring me bags."

He attacked the room like a little tornado. No sentimental conflicts for him. He threw away all the empty Lego boxes, the 365 calendar pages, the ski ticket from 1977, the vintage lumps of orange clay from the second grade, the used lunch bag collection, and the gum wrappers. He filled two garbage cans with debris, rated it a "slightly satisfying experience," and pocketed his money.

There were many benefits to the plan. The room got cleaned. I didn't go crazy. And everybody could relax for the few remaining days of summer.

Furthermore, the organizer has a mind like a steel trap. For the next year we could ask him things like, "Does your brother have his bike lock in there?" and he would know.

"Yup—top dresser drawer under the socks."

I asked him later how he had managed to get rid of so much stuff without infuriating his brother.

"Oh it was easy," he said, proudly snapping the rubber bands on his braces like suspenders. "I told him to look in the bags for the stuff he wanted to save but he never did. So I just threw it all out."

He warned me, however, that he had not realized the full extent of the job and that his prices would go up next year. But I don't mind. It's worth it. Maybe next year we would even have a picnic, go to the beach, or enjoy an ice cream cone.

And I don't think $20 is too much for that.

# COMMANDO TACTICS
# FOR KIDDIE CLUTTER

Parents, is your child's room strewn with pieces of Mr. Potato Head, fossilized Play-Doh, homework from three grades back, and hundreds of miscellaneous items that defy classification?

Are the piles of dirty clothes beginning to take on a personality of their own? Are there enough clothes spread out to dress an entire Third World Nation?

Well, parents, take heart. We down at Children's Rooms Control Systems (CRCS) have the answer for you.

We have a line of six custom options from which to choose, each one guaranteed to make your child's room a place you wouldn't mind showing your mother-in-law, or the entire PTA for that matter.

So call or stop in today and choose a plan that can restore order and civil communication at your house.

THE VITO OPTION. Here, we send a dark, burly man to visit your son or daughter. He stands in the doorway of the room, cracking his knuckles, and simply says, "I want this room clean by sundown. You dig?" Have rags and cleaning supplies handy; your child will come barrelling out begging for them in no time. Vito works best with children under ten.

THE RELIGIOUS CHORUS. A group of five men and women come into your home and chant and pray over your child's room until it is clean. This option has been known to cause miracles; works best with children over ten.

THE SUC-VAC OPTION. This option is for times of true parental desperation. Mounted on a truck, the patented Suc-Vac will clean your child's room in seconds, leaving no messy traces. This is designed for the child who has never thrown or put anything away in his or her life. We recommend you give your child a small bag and five minutes to save anything of value to them. Then Bert, our driver, will back the truck up to your house and clamp the door-shaped nozzle onto your child's room. In no time, your child's room will be spotless, ready for another decade of abuse. The Suc-Vac will pick up anything including dust balls, entire Lego cities, and hair mousse cans.

MAGIC SAW. Surely you've fantasized about this. For a small fortune, you can have your dream come true. Have one of our technicians, all of whom are named Marvin, come to your home and actually saw around the edges of your child's room, letting it fall cleanly away from the house. No muss, no fuss. Marvin even vacuums up the sawdust. Optional feature: Max the backhoe operator will carve out a hole the size of a volcano crater in your yard for the room to rest in. Fill over with dirt and seed and you can have grass growing within ten days to two weeks.

THE CHEMICAL OPTION. When your child is at school or camp, let one of our trained technicians spray the room and its contents with our miracle high-fiber spray. In one hour, this special substance returns every bit of matter in your child's room—animal, mineral, vegetable or whatever—to its original state. The dust-to-dust alternative.

Einstein developed the formula for this substance when he was trying to figure out how to clean up his niece's room.

BURGLARY. When you plan your next vacation, let us arrange for our team of trained cat burglars to enter your home and remove everything and anything from your child's room, including broken aquariums and unused weight-lifting sets. Just let your kids try and pin that on you!

So parents, remember. We down at Children's Rooms Control Systems can help you find peace of mind. And be assured, recent court cases have ruled our methods do not constitute child abuse.

As a final bonus, call us within the next two weeks and receive absolutely free of charge a portable mess detector. Worn just like a beeper it alerts you, no matter where you are or what you are doing, whenever a piece of laundry or a gum wrapper hits the floor. And for a small maintenance charge, you can have Vito or the Religious Chorus make monthly house calls for further motivation and upkeep.

Call us today, parents, and sleep well tonight.

# YOUR (BLIP) WAFFLES
# ARE (BLEEP) READY!

My husband had been hiding the computer magazines under our bed for almost a year.

"If the kids find out I'm even thinking about buying a computer, they'll bug me endlessly," he explained.

"But do I really need a computer?" he'd moan late at night after the kids had gone to bed.

Ever since he was eight years old and his mother made him return a cap gun to the store—"She thought I should save my money"—it's been almost impossible for him to spend money on anything other than basic necessities, like groceries and lawn fertilizer.

But finally, he convinced himself that a computer was a basic necessity. He rationalized the purchase by imagining the kids would gravitate to programs teaching algebra or French. Maybe they'd even learn to program, he would muse.

When he broke the news to the kids they said, "Ah ha! We thought so. Why else would you be keeping *Computer Times* and *Computer World* under your bed?"

We eschewed the discount stores (they were all sold out) in favor of an outfit which provided two hours of free instruction.

While those two hours were probably a blessing, I went on overload after the first twenty minutes. I read once that we can only hold seven new ideas in our minds at one time, and I'd reached my limit. Of those seven, I only remember two: I learned how to "pop the top off" the computer, although why I would want to do this, I don't know, and that the basic guts, the really important part, the MAIN PART is called the "Mother Board." I like this.

The three of them set up the computer at home, as per instructions. Then while my husband and I made dinner, the boys worked together to figure out how to play our one game, thrown in free, called "Galactic Saga."

When we summoned them to dinner, they screamed they couldn't come. They were waiting for a message.

"From whom?" I demanded.

"From the messenger, of course."

"Well, here's the message: Get down here this instant!"

They sat down at the table; their cheeks pink, their eyes glazed. "We finally had a chance of winning," they said accusingly.

When we awoke the next morning, they were already in the den-turned-computer-room. They ate breakfast in shifts so one could man the game and frantically search the manual to find out how to stop a game in the middle. (That turned out to be Push Q).

When I complained about the time they were spending, one son consoled me with: "Look at it this way—we're learning a lot about military planning.

"Really, it's degrading," he continued, "to be working on an intricate battle plan and hear, 'Your waffles are ready.'"

After they consumed Galactic Whatever, they turned into criminals and broke copyright laws borrowing and copying games from other people—grownups and kids alike. They stayed at the computer day and night. An eerie silence hung over the room, broken only by little squirrely noises escaping from under the door.

"Does a robot have you at bay in there?" I would ask, amused at my wit. They never answered.

Periodically I went in to make human contact and to check their pulses, which were usually racing.

Once the computer screen said, "Resurrection Unsuccessful."

"What does that mean?" I asked.

"Leave me alone, will you?"

"But wait—that's a religious term. What's it doing . . . "

"Thanks a lot," he hissed. "You just made me get killed."

A fine layer of perspiration had broken out all over his face. No wonder his brother complains about sweat on the joystick. I sensed my usefulness was over and I slipped quietly from the room.

The next time he was more cheerful. "Let me show you this. See the little men coming down in parachutes? You can shoot their parachutes off and they die a gruesome death," he chuckled. We watched as a little green stick figure exploded into smithereens.

And he'd always been such a kind boy.

A few weeks later, when our wedding anniversary came around, the boys urged us to go out. It wasn't out of any concern for our well-being. We could hear them scheduling the evening into hours and assigning equal computer time.

When it was time to go, I discovered that my husband of seventeen years had been closeted in a sweaty room for three hours, trying to program a blip to go in circles on the computer screen.

After I threatened him with the D word, he came to, showered and changed his clothes. Once in the car he told me, "Don't worry. It will pass and fall into its proper perspective . . . just as soon as I get the little ball to bounce around the screen."

He could tell by the look on my face that I didn't find this funny. After awhile, I said, "Oh well. I'll get my revenge." I took out my pencil. "Now let's see, how old were you when your mother made you return that cap gun?"

# DURAN DURAN!
## MUST YOU, MUST YOU?

It was a typical Sunday afternoon; twenty projects started, none completed; newspapers were strewn all over the family room.

The phone rang. It was for our oldest son, who is sixteen.

He put his hand over the phone. "Can I go to a rock concert?"

My husband and I looked at each other. "Why us? Why now?"

"We'll have to talk about it," we told him.

"But he needs to know right this minute," he insisted. "The first day is already sold out."

We held firm.

He hung up and looked surly. "You'd better be a little more friendly," we told him in an unfriendly fashion, "or we won't let you go at all."

"This is as friendly as I can be," he said in a strained voice.

We grilled him: "Where is it? Who's playing? How will you get there and back?"

"The Oakland Coliseum. Duran Duran. Somebody's parents will take us to the BART Station and pick us up when it's over."

I looked at him. He is almost six feet tall. He is probably old enough and big enough to go to a rock concert. But was I ready?

I grasped at straws: "Don't you know people have been trampled to death at rock concerts?" and "I read a man was stabbed recently in a BART parking lot."

He looked at me as if I had just flown in from Mars. "Don't have a psychotic episode, Mom."

I grilled his brother, who is fourteen. "Who is this group? Are they reasonable? Do they kill chickens on stage?"

He reassured me they were OK and reminded me we'd bought his brother a record of said group last Christmas.

Later, I sneaked up to my son's bedroom and scrutinized the album cover. Duran Duran appeared to be a group of disgruntled looking youths with short hair, wearing tuxedos. At least they were wearing clothes.

I read the list of songs. One was called, "Looking for Cracks in the Pavement."

I decided to listen. As soon as the needle hit the record, a tribal beat issued forth. Suddenly I thought of my father who always described the 50s rock and roll I loved as so much "banging and pounding, pounding and banging."

When the voices started, it sounded like the singers had a bad case of hiccups in unison.

My husband walked in and listened for a few minutes. "Sounds like they're beating a monkey to death," he observed and wandered out, his hands over his ears.

Later my husband and I went for a walk to discuss the newest wrinkle in living with teenagers. We decided to let him go. He said he had the money for a ticket, and we liked the friends he'd be going with.

When we told him of our decision, he kept his face immobile and said, "Thanks," dryly. Looking at him, I thought no one would bother him on BART. Still, I wished I'd enrolled him in jujitsu classes when he was younger.

The late night trip on BART kept bothering me.

"Hey, I have an idea," I told him. "I'll go along and write about it, like an undercover journalist."

The look he gave me could peel wallpaper off the wall.

"If you go, Mom, I'm not going."

Later that evening we overheard him trying to squeeze six dollars out of his younger brother, who has been known to invest his money in the stock market and has repeatedly stated that "rock concerts are dumb."

His brother didn't lend him the money and he never asked us. "He's probably embarrassed because he said he had the money," said my husband, who has to explain the macho consciousness to me.

The next day we asked about the ticket. "They were already sold out," he said, looking at us pointedly.

We heaved a sigh of relief and settled back into our psychic easy chairs.

Not long afterwards, our younger son came into the room. He sat down. "Mom, Dad? There's a rock concert coming up, with a group called Yes. Do you think I could go and invite a friend?"

Oh no. Will they never quit?

"I know," I said, perking up. "I'll go with you. I'll write about it. It will be an experience."

His face fell. "Nah, forget it. I don't think I really want to go anyway."

I think I'm on to something here.

# A NEW DRIVER

There are some things for which we are never fully prepared. Take the case of the first born child receiving a driver's license.

Precisely one hour before he was due at the DMV, our son said, "Oh, by the way, I need my birth certificate."

After a frenzied search of the desk drawers, file cabinets and wastepaper baskets, I concluded his birth certificate was entombed in the safety deposit box. At the bank. Which wouldn't open for another hour.

He fiddled with the driver's manual. "Maybe I don't need it after all," he mumbled, with no certitude whatsoever.

I ripped the little booklet out of his hands and scanned the fine print. We agreed he could probably get by with a passport, which fortunately he had. But not before I wanted to say nasty things like, "And you think you're ready to drive a car?"

His father accompanied him to the DMV while I stayed home to recover my wits.

Just my luck—he passed. And on the last day of summer vacation our son became a Driver.

"Can I invite a friend for lunch and take the car?" he said, the second he walked in the house.

After a quick phone call, he came to me, hand outstretched, and announced, "I need money and the car keys."

As I watched him drive down the street, I remembered the first day he toddled off to kindergarten wearing his little red cowboy hat. Today he was wearing sunglasses on a leash.

Was he driving out of my life forever? Was I ready? For a moment I really wanted that little boy in his red cowboy hat back.

While he was gone, unpreparedness struck again. "Oh no. What about insurance?" I blurted out loud. I answered myself. "I hope there's a thirty-day grace period."

"What's that?" asked my other son, the non-driver, who had to content himself having lunch with mom until such time as he could escape with the car.

"Well do you know what grace is?" I asked. He thought he did.

"Well you have it for thirty days," I finished.

We ate the rest of our lunch in silence while I contemplated the concept of grace.

But this was nothing compared to the first time my son drove on the freeway. I was in my creative writing class at the time he would be on the big road. All sorts of creative and horrible thoughts pierced my brain. On ramps, off ramps, other drivers, big trucks. Would he be fiddling with the radio or the tape player? How could I ever be ready for this? Why was I even trying to be a writer? If I were any kind of a mother I'd be home ready to drive my son everywhere in an armored vehicle. I knew I was acting crazy, but I couldn't help it.

Then one woman read a story about a mother whose child had died. I couldn't stop crying. Everyone began staring at me and edging away.

Finally at break time I ran to the pay phone. How could I face it if anything happened to him I wondered, as I dialed our number.

I was relieved when he answered the phone. He was

fine. But I would never believe what happened. On the way home, a car rear ended another car right in front of him. Fortunately he'd learned to leave a lot of room between himself and the car ahead.

"So I tapped my brakes to signal the drivers behind me and then slowed down," he reported. He was able to avoid the accident and still had the presence of mind to notice the obscene gestures the two drivers flashed at each other.

After that, I decided to go on the offensive to prepare for any and all contingencies.

Early Sunday morning, I woke my husband from a sound sleep. Dressed in combat fatigues and boots, I marched my sleepy son and husband out to the car.

"Show him how to change flat tires," I ordered.

He did. They located the tools, discussed the condition of the spares, and practiced jacking up the car.

I consulted my clipboard. "Now talk about tire pressure."

They consulted stickers and books. My husband showed him the tire wear test using a Lincoln penny.

"Now discuss oil and water."

They opened the hood, peered in, and unscrewed various caps and inserted sticks into the engine innards.

Confident that our first born was now initiated into the mysteries of cars, I allowed him and my husband to return to their regular Sunday activities.

As I followed them into the house, the full weight of what we had done struck me. We had just shown our baby how to change a tire. I suddenly saw him out on the busy freeway, struggling with jacks and bolts while a drunk driver careened into him.

I found my husband pouring himself a cup of coffee. "Do you really expect him to change a tire?" I asked.

"Yup," he said, simply.

This was a new thought. I mean I've seen the Tire Changing Demonstration lots of times but in no case did I ever really expect to change a tire. I'm sure my father never expected me to change a tire. What had I done?

I located my son. He was listening to his album of The Cars (I did not make this up) and reading the funnies. "Come with me," I whispered. He peeled himself reluctantly off the bed and followed me into the bedroom. I shut the door.

"This is how you change a tire," I said. I opened the phone book and showed him where to find Tow Truck in the yellow pages.

"And always carry a quarter."

"Oh Mom," was all he said before he turned on his sneaker and left.

I fell to my knees. "Oh God, I'm not ready for this," I wailed.

God answered back. "Oh yes you are. You have to be.

"You don't have any choice."

# TEEN PERKS

"It must be wild, having teenagers," a woman with three children under the age of ten once said to me.

But really, it's not nearly as wild as three children under the age of ten. In fact, it occurred to me that parents receive a lot of perks when their offspring reach teenagedom.

For one thing, people in their teens make their own lunches. No more giggly, restless toying with the balanced repast you've prepared, or running out in the backyard when you're not looking to feed it to the rabbit. By the time they hit adolescence, they've seen the charts with the basic food groups and know about fat and cholesterol. All I need to do is stock the refrigerator and stand back.

Even better, they go out and buy their own clothing (with your money, of course). My days of driving them to the malls and sitting outside the dressing rooms are over. In fact, teenagers don't even want you in the stores with them. You've become an embarrassment. I knew I was truly finished with this stage of my life when my son rented his prom tuxedo without me.

Laundry is another fringe benefit. They do their own. They insist on it. Only they know how to shrink their jeans just right and which shirts can't go in the dryer.

But the most liberating thing about teenagers is that they can drive themselves, and their brothers, to dentist appointments, music lessons, and the like. No longer is my life built around orthodontist appointments!

Of course, there is no free lunch. The down side of teenagers driving is that as they are gaining experience, they can and do have car accidents. I guess there's a price for everything.

Another wonderful thing about teenagers is that they don't need babysitters. Well, actually they do, but try and find someone. Thus parents feel a certain amount of freedom in going away for a few nights all by themselves. No longer do your children cry or pout when you go out. In fact they are very encouraging.

"You're going away? Great! For how long? One week? How about two? Have a good time. Enjoy yourselves. Don't hurry back."

Teenagers also have developed a sense of humor which, if they choose to share it with you, can be hilarious. The days of my feigned amusement over silly jokes are over. Some days I feel like I'm living on the set of "Saturday Night Live."

But one of the very best parts about older kids is that they know what they want to do, more or less, and you don't have to try and figure it out for them.

When our children were growing up, we often felt burdened with impossible decisions for which there were no clear-cut answers: Should they sign up for soccer camp or take music lessons? Drama productions or overnight camp? When to push and when to let go?

Now they tell us what they want to do. There's no way you can choose for them, and there's a certain amount of relief that comes with that.

It's not that they no longer need parents, but our role shifts from one of director (dictator, my kids would say) to more of an assistant and sometime flunky.

Occasionally parents are called upon to pick up the pieces, or dispense Band-Aids and sympathy. Or live through certain embarrassing ordeals which all teenagers put their parents through. I'm sworn to secrecy, but let me say I've had dealings with certain authority figures I would never have heard from if it hadn't been for certain young people I know and love.

Yes, it is nice to have older kids. I can't think of a single bad thing about it, except that to them you rank, on the social and intelligence scale, slightly above a banana slug.

And that our only remaining avenue of puny influence seems to be low-key suggestions, which I use frequently, but generally to no avail. I know, and they know, that I can no longer "make" them do anything, nor do I (really) want to. Well maybe sometimes, but I can't. So I don't humiliate myself by trying.

But most of the time it turns out that they were right all along and it was you who were off base.

And that is oddly comforting. For you realize they are going to be OK without you. And you no longer have to be the wise and all-knowing parents you once were.

Or thought you were.

# HOUSE
# AND
# GARDEN

# LIFE WITHOUT PRUNE WHIP

"The woman who spends time reading and collecting recipes she'll never use is engaging in futile behavior." So sayeth time management expert Alan Lakein in his book *How to Get Control of Your Time and Your Life.* Furthermore, he hints darkly, such a woman is using up valuable time which could be spent in productive activities such as actually cooking for her family.

His words leaped out at me because I have indulged in this frivolous and futile activity ever since I got married and began collecting recipes and cookbooks.

I find pleasure in pulling out my *Fanny Farmer Cookbook* and reading recipes for Peg's Molasses Cookies, Cucumber Tea Sandwiches, or Chicken Pie. I also enjoy clipping recipes from magazines and newspapers and taping them onto cards in my alphabetized recipe file box. Although I don't make many of these dishes, I feel better knowing that somewhere, someone else is.

It's not that I don't want to spend hours cooking for my family. I grew up in the 1950s and know that Mom's job is in the kitchen turning out food, creating the glue that holds a happy family together. But over the years I discovered that if I spent too much time in the kitchen fiddling with too many ingredients, I became hostile to that very family I was trying to preserve. So I turned to recipe reading and collecting as a satisfying substitute.

But one afternoon I decided to face facts, seize control of my time and my life, and purge myself of these useless recipes. I faced down the cabinet packed with cookbooks, pamphlets, bent and twisted recipe cards, and yellowed newspaper clippings.

I attacked my overstuffed file box. Some of the clipped recipes had been around so long the tape on the cards had evaporated and the recipes had fallen off and turned to dust.

I discovered I had collected twenty-five recipes for pumpkin pie. Now let's be frank here. I have made pumpkin pie twice in my life. Once, I used the recipe on the back of the canned pumpkin and once I slaughtered a real pumpkin "for the experience." But it never occurred to me to consult my file box for a recipe.

My second most popular choice were recipes for homey sounding varieties of pot roast, each to be "rounded out nicely" with a loaf of crusty French bread and a green salad. Funny, the recipe I always used—the one where you slather a hunk of meat with cream of mushroom soup, dry onion soup mix, and a splash of red wine, and leave the whole thing in a slow oven for five hours—wasn't even in there. I began to wonder if I was leading some kind of double life.

I pitched all the recipes for homemade bread, including brown bread, dilly bread, and bread baked in coffee and tennis ball cans. I also threw out the pictures I'd saved of two hands and a lump of white dough, illustrating how to reap the ecstatic pleasures of kneading. I had to face facts: I was as likely to bake my own bread as I was to take up parachute jumping.

I saved the cards which classified as historical documents: a recipe for applesauce cake written in a tidy, girlish printing by my once best friend, Melanie; instructions written in my own twelve-year-old shaky cursive for a 50s delicacy called Peach Marlow (featuring marshmallows and canned peaches); and a card printed in tall letters by my son when he was nine for a concoction featuring chocolate chips and Cheerios.

Flinging out the directions for apple blintzes, which rambled on for three cards, both sides, and recipes for making my own salad dressings, I left my newly thinned file box and confronted the cookbooks.

I pulled out a collection of recipes from members of a church in Pennsylvania. I have never lived in Pennsylvania. I have no idea how I came to own this book. I glanced through to make sure I wasn't missing anything. The first recipe was for Easy Raised Rolls. Lies! From a church yet! Just whom do they think they're kidding? Skimming the index I found Prune Whip. I thought "prune whip" was a punch line to a joke about hospital food. Burger Bundles. I couldn't bear to read the ingredients. Potato Chip and Tuna Casserole. Now who needs the recipe for that? Western Beef Tots. I peeked. Hamburger, cream of mushroom soup and—you guessed it— Tater Tots. Gagging, I let Pennsylvania hit the garbage bag.

I picked up a cookbook for Chinese food. I bought this after reading an article in a woman's magazine about a mother who fed her large, healthy family on six cents a day and entertained on eight cents. Her secret? Chinese food. By shredding one pork chop she claimed she could create a feast for twelve big eaters. I tossed it with the full knowledge that I will never shred a pork chop.

Once I got into it, the recipe tossing took on a life of its own. I grabbed the Gourmet Blender Cookbook. The first recipe bordered on the pornographic. Calling for boned chicken breasts, it instructed the cook to "run the filets through the meat grinder, then put in blender with whipping cream and white of one egg." It suggested cutting out six heart-shaped pieces of parchment paper on which to serve the breasts.

Suddenly this reminded me of a local murder case. A woman had killed her husband and cut him up and cooked him in their backyard barbecue. Had phrases like "run the filets through the meat grinder" given her ideas?

As I dove deeper and deeper into the cabinet, I came across a cookbook, *Busy Little Hands,* featuring that old family favorite, crepe paper paste.

By the time I'd filled two grocery bags with discards, I was laughing wildly, calling out to anyone within earshot. "Hey listen to this—Barbecued Pig's Feet, Eggplant Ratatouille, Creamed Leeks, Quince Nutlets, Pumpkin Pecan Pie...." Hey, wait a minute. That one sounds pretty good.

Maybe I'll save it. One recipe can't hurt, can it? Besides, it will make such good reading on a crisp, fall afternoon.

# THE THRILL OF GROCERIES

I have always hated grocery shopping. Frankly, I prefer having my teeth drilled, close to the nerve. It's the choices and details that drive me crazy, as well as a deep-rooted belief, as I sort through miles of boxes, bottles and cans, that I am wasting my entire life.

But for almost twenty years, I dutifully trundled off to the grocery store each week, my face set into the look of someone about to be executed.

Sometimes my husband stood in the doorway, waved, and said cheerily, "Have a good time."

"I never have a good time at the grocery store," I'd snap.

After he had his consciousness raised, he said annoying things like, "It's your choice but remember—you create your own experience."

It was then I decided to take him up on his long-standing offer to do the grocery shopping.

The first time he went to the store, he put on his sneakers and strapped on his Sony Walkman, ready to bebop down the aisles in time to country music.

He returned two hours later. It took all four of us running in relay for half an hour just to transport the goods into the house.

I looked into one bag. "Twelve cans of tuna?"

"They were having a sale," he said, waving his hands.

"Six TV dinners?"

"Yes, they're handy to have around."

"Don't you know they're poison? Did you read the list of additives? Haven't you heard about the sodium in these things?"

He looked at me as if I were a lunatic. But then he doesn't have the twenty-year history I do of reading about the health hazards lurking in almost every food.

He pulled out two large economy-sized packages of egg noodles. "I figured with you going back to school, we'd be having a lot of tuna casseroles."

Was he trying to make me feel guilty or what?

In silence, we put away the bottles of soda, the potato chips, and the sugary cereals. The kids hung around drooling and saying things like, "Pretzels, ohhh, peanuts, ahhh."

I felt as if my two-decade struggle trying to serve my family Wholesome Foods was being tossed down the garbage disposal by an insensitive lout wearing a Walkman.

We emptied another bag—five boxes of frozen waffles. "For quick breakfasts," he said cheerily. I stifled my urge to point out the aluminum in them and the possible connection to Alzheimer's disease.

A big bag of M & Ms, a pound of pistachios, and five grapefruit to add to the five already softening in the refrigerator.

"Where are the apples and the celery and lettuce I had on the list?" I asked.

"Oh, I didn't have room for them," he said. "I'll get them next time."

Finally the last bag was folded and put away. "How much did you spend?" I asked.

"$146," he said proudly.

I thought that was incredible, considering the only meat he'd purchased were two packages of chicken legs and a pound of hamburger.

"I don't know how you did it," I said.

"Thank you," he replied modestly.

The next day my son came to me and complained there was nothing to eat.

"Nothing to eat? Your father spent $146 on groceries and you tell me there's nothing to eat?"

"It was hog heaven for a day, but now there's nothing," he said. And what he really wanted was an apple.

I suppose I'll have to go back to doing the grocery shopping. I hate to take the fun away from him though. He told me he found it "thrilling" to do the grocery shopping. He loved the freedom of running up and down the aisles, listening to music, and grabbing things off the shelves.

I think he's acting out his boyhood fantasies from the years he spent deprived of junk food by a Mom with a degree in Home Economics. He's told me he didn't taste white bread until he went away to college. He had chocolate about once a year. And he was the only kid in his elementary school who didn't have store-bought cupcakes in his lunch.

I guess I'll have to wrest the shopping cart from his hands. I can't overcome the force of a childhood deprived of junk food.

Sigh. Back to wasting my life. Although now I appreciate my efforts a little more. After all, I did manage to raise a kid who actually wanted an apple.

Now that's an accomplishment.

# ARE MICROWAVES MORAL?

When you ask people about their microwave ovens, responses fall into two categories. Some folks shrug and say, "I only use it for warming leftovers and reheating coffee." Others cross themselves and murmur reverently, "I couldn't live without mine."

I came to the world of microwaves late, but I had three good reasons for not plunging into the New Wave of cooking. I didn't want to give up precious counter space to a black box; I hated the thought of having to spend time learning new ways to cook; and I knew microwave ovens definitely caused cancer.

My husband, the electrical engineer, scoffed at my fear of microwaves.

"They're only radio waves," he said. "They're in the air all around us."

"Sure, sure," I said, humoring him.

"Do you worry about the waves when you listen to the radio or watch TV?" he asked.

I countered with scientific fact. "Well how come if you put a hamster in the microwave, it will explode, huh, huh?"

"Well, of course, if you put your hand in there it will hurt you," he admitted.

But safety considerations aside, the more I read, the more tempting a microwave sounded.

The fact that they cooked food in a quarter of the

time needed by a conventional oven sounded perfect. I was ready for fast. Studies show modern women spend twenty-one hours a week on meals—buying, cooking, cleaning up. If I whittled that down a bit, I could do something really swell. Like deflea the cat or paint my toenails.

But speed was just one of the features. I was astounded to discover a microwave lets you cook in serving dishes!

Cook in serving dishes! No more pots and pans! When I mentioned this to my sons, who do pot scrubbing duty twice a week, they whooped and gave each other high fives.

The further I read, the juicier it got. The heck with serving dishes. In a microwave, you can cook on paper towels, paper napkins, and in plastic bags! An ear of corn cooks in its own husk! An artichoke in plastic wrap! Oatmeal in a bowl! Popcorn in a bag! Coffee in a cup! Bacon on a paper plate!!!

How had I missed all this?

And defrosting. "The microwave defrosts in a twinkling of an eye," said the literature. Never again to be faced with an intransigent block of frozen hamburger while the kids are hollering they need to eat in five minutes.

My mind reeled. This was too good to be true. There had to be something wrong.

What about the younger generation? What would replace the character-building activities of scrubbing burned fat out of a greasy pan and chipping dried tuna bake out of a casserole?

How, if you can have a baked potato in five minutes or a burrito in three, will young people ever learn patience or develop the skills necessary for long-range planning? What ever happened to delayed gratification? Wasn't that supposed to be good for you?

And what would happen to me if I had the capability to

cook bacon without having to clean up a greasy pan? Would I become decadent, not to mention chubby?

But the pluses outweighed the minuses. I relinquished my moral considerations along with my counter space and embraced the world of microwaves.

After we purchased, I realized the microwave oven comes with a built-in potential to induce guilt.

At a cooking demonstration the instructor said, "Since the microwave doesn't heat up the kitchen, you can even make lasagne on a very hot day."

My husband looked at me with large puppy dog eyes.

"Forget it," I snapped. "I am not going to buy a microwave so I can fool around with lasagne on a very hot day."

And I had to ignore the hype in the operating manual. "When dinner takes so little time, you'll make fewer trips to the Burger Palace." I didn't want to give up any trips to the Burger Palace.

But aside from the guilt feature, I'm rapidly turning into a starry-eyed convert.

Of course I have to consult maps, charts and calculators every time I cook something new. And learning to work the digital control panel has been traumatic, given my past failure experiences with programming the VCR.

But it's all worth it. Cooking is fun again. I love cooking on paper napkins and in plastic bags. I feel as if I'm really getting away with something.

One book described the microwave oven with its radio waves as a "miniature broadcasting system."

It's definitely playing my song.

# PLAGUED BY PEACHES

In the late 60s, we bought a tract house in an area of California that had once been an apricot orchard. Each tiny yard inherited one apricot tree. Coming from the East, we were completely unprepared for the lavish productivity of the California soil. We were shocked when on July 5, 1969, 10,000 small, orange, globes became ripe, softened and fell onto our lawn within fifteen minutes. Every summer I struggled to find ways to render apricots edible to my family. I always failed. When the tree finally died, I wasn't sad.

You would think we had learned our lesson, but no. The next year we planted a twig that the nursery man swore was a peach tree.

The first summer the slender shoot presented us with two perfect peaches. The second year, our darling tree blessed us with sixteen luscious pieces of fruit.

This year the damn thing has showered us with upwards of two hundred peaches and is still going strong.

There are peaches on the ground. There are peaches in the pool. Peaches lurk on every inch of my kitchen table and counters, in stages from unripe to rotten. Even the refrigerator is packed with what once was my favorite fruit.

I am developing a cavalier attitude toward these proliferating fuzz factories. If one rolls onto the floor, I throw it away. If I cut into one and it's not perfectly ripe, too bad—I fling it from me. Nibbled by insects? Heave it.

That still leaves me with more peaches than I can stuff into my family. But not for lack of trying.

In an attempt to be reasonable, I approached the plague of peaches as a mathematical problem. I informed family members that if each one of them cooperated and consumed seven peaches a day, we could clear out the kitchen, yard, and pool within a week.

They refused. They said they only wanted to eat peaches "when they felt like it," which meant about once a week.

"Why don't you Make Things?" asked my older son.

"Like what?"

"You know, pies and stuff. Cobbler. Like Grandma would."

"Hey kid," I told him. "We women aren't into that scene anymore. We've been liberated. Where have you been?"

"Where have you been?" countered the teenager. "Things have changed again. Even Geraldine Ferraro admits she makes blueberry muffins. And Gloria Steinem is wearing mini skirts and contact lenses. Face it, Mom. Liberation is dead."

I suppose he has a point. I could Make Things. But I made that mistake with the apricots. And sanity is held by such a slender thread.

Although no one in our family liked apricots, during the harvest, I stayed in the kitchen for days into long nights making apricot jam, which we rarely ate; soggy apricot pies, which we never ate; and apricot and walnut squares which even the dog wouldn't sniff and the garbage disposal couldn't swallow.

One year, I really flipped out and attempted to make something featured in *Sunset Magazine* called "Apricot Leather." I still don't know what apricot leather is supposed to look or taste like, but I do know it is the strongest adhesive known to woman. Bits of the orange stuff are still embedded in my linoleum.

I'm wiser now. I know that if I go into that kitchen and start looking up peach recipes, I'll get involved with one of those Fanny Farmer numbers that reads, "Take twenty-four perfect peaches; dip them rapidly in boiling water; peel quickly." Then immerse them in sterilized glass jars in a concoction of fifteen ingredients I don't have.

Next, I'll decide that since I'm already in the kitchen, one peach pie wouldn't hurt. Then I'll be looking up recipes for atrocities like peach 'n wheat germ muffins, which no one will ever eat, and in no time I'll be up to the ceiling in sticky pots and pans.

Then some kid will come into the kitchen to get a snack, (not a peach), and I will go berserk and find fault with that kid's walk, talk and the way he drips water on the floor. And if not led away, I will soon be calling him names and ordering him to clean up his room this instant.

So for the good of mankind, or at least the mankind that lives at my house, I am refraining from becoming overly involved with the peaches.

Fortunately, my neighbor, who is also from the East Coast, found a good way to use the apricots when we were in the apricot business, and I think it will work with peaches.*

Meanwhile, my husband tells me if the current projections hold up, next year that tree could produce 4,000 pieces of fruit.

I'm wondering how peach wood burns. I hear it makes a lovely fire.

---

*Recipe for Peach Nectar: Peel and cut up one quart of peaches. Add one quart of cold water. Boil for five minutes and cool briefly. Whirl in blender; add one half cup sugar and one tablespoon lemon juice. Pour into glass containers and freeze. Leave in freezer for five years, then throw away.

# PLANT MANIA

I like spring as much as the next person. But I do have to guard against the season's greatest pitfall: plant mania, an irrational desire to put plants into the earth.

We are all victims of biology. The increased hours of daylight activate our gardening hormones which, like our appendix, have no function. They were rendered obsolete with the invention of the grocery store.

Unfortunately, writers of garden articles do not understand this. Each year they extol the wonders of planting and harvesting backyard crops. I'm not completely immune to their promises of produce. But every time I'm tempted to grow my own corn or sow eight varieties of lettuce in a half barrel, I stop and remember the strawberries.

A few years ago I was hooked by an article, complete with vivid illustrations, about planting strawberries. All I had to do was stick the plants into the ground and, as long as I cut off the runners, I would have a bumper crop of "luscious berries." There was even a coupon from a local nursery offering me a dozen plants for a quarter.

I skipped to the store to cash in my coupon. In my excitement, I failed to notice the shelves of pesticide, insecticide, bags of Supersoil, Wonderbark, perlite, vermiculite, hose attachments, root feeders, and bird nets lurking ominously in the background.

At home, I gathered my gardening implements and

proceeded to the back yard. A quick read of the directions informed me strawberries liked soil that was well drained and rich. Heavy clay soil like mine required liberal doses of steer manure and redwood compost. And vermiculite for aeration.

I returned to the nursery where I discovered the needed ingredients were sold only in quantities that would last a lifetime. Driven by images of "luscious berries," I bought the farm.

Back home I tried not to dwell on the origins of steer manure as I hacked away at our impenetrable clay soil. After several hours, I managed to reduce the dirt clods into clumps the size of tennis balls. Then I twirled in manure and compost. The area looked like it had been hit with hand grenades.

Next, I read that strawberries like to be planted in mounds 5 to 6 inches high, 14 to 16 inches apart and positioned at a 21 degree angle perpendicular to the moon.

I marched into the house for a slide rule, compass and yardstick. These plants were beginning to get on my nerves with all their "needs."

Finally, it was time to plant. I tried to keep those little strawberry crowns above the soil line, as the directions advised, to avoid the perils of crown rot. But it was difficult since I was planting them on a slope.

Just as I was administering the vitamin solution with an eyedropper (to ward off root shock), my husband came out of the house.

"You planted them too deep," he said.

I tried to straighten up to scream and shake my fist at him, but my back was so stiff, I couldn't move. It took all my strength to whisper, "I don't care and shut up."

My visions of strawberry shortcake and strawberry pie and sliced strawberries on vanilla ice cream were fading and being replaced by a growing awareness of my own stiff body and possibly reduced life span.

The tyrannical directions next told me I should tuck straw under the plants to keep the berries off the ground. Unfortunately, in suburbia, straw is in short supply. I read on and discovered the straw also provided "mulch." If I didn't have straw, I could use sawdust. Great. Another substance rarely found in suburbia.

Finally, I discovered I could use black plastic. Now black plastic was something I had. Like a woman possessed, I cut up my black plastic garbage bags into neat little circles. Then I snipped out holes in the centers and fitted them over the tiny plants like clown collars or baby bibs.

"What are you doing?" my husband asked, from his position on the patio.

"Never mind. You wouldn't believe it if I told you."

While he was watching, a gentle wind came up and blew the plastic over the plants like little capes.

I searched the yard for rocks to keep the plastic on the ground. But through years of landscaping, my husband had systematically removed every rock and pebble from our yard.

I grabbed some small sticks from the woodpile and plunged them into the plastic. This worked for awhile, until I tried to water the plants. It was impossible to get water under black plastic that is stabbed into the ground.

My husband finally quit watching me when I pointed one of these sticks at him. He slunk back into the house.

After a few weeks, when I was able to walk without much trace of a limp, I went out and checked on the plants. The plastic seemed to be frying the tender green leaves into dry bits.

I ripped off my handiwork.

In time, strawberries did arrive. But so did the snails. I

was rarely able to pick a berry that hadn't already been sampled. Somehow, once a snail has chewed on a strawberry, I'm no longer interested.

Some heavy duty number crunching at the kitchen table revealed to me that I had shelled out approximately $50 on those plants, not counting potential doctor bills, yet all I had accomplished was to provide a free lunch for snails and affordable housing for slugs.

If I'd bought strawberries at the grocery store at a dollar a pint, I'd have had 50 pints. As it was, we ended up with 10 perfect berries, or $5 per. And no strawberry is that good.

Now those fanatic garden writers will tell you that even though gardening is not always cost effective, it is "life enhancing." To that, I say, "steer manure."

Growing one's own food is an ancient, barbaric custom and I, for one, intend to overcome my primitive destiny and evolve to a higher plane.

But one has to be careful. It's turning toward spring and the garden writers are at it again trying to entrap their victims. In today's newspaper, a headline prophesies, "Tomato Adventures Start in February." The caption below the picture tells me I can grow orange and yellow hybrid tomatoes, and even ones with stripes.

I turn the page and read about how I can grow a salad of arugula, chicory, red mustard, and curly cress in a basket in two weeks.

It's tempting but I must be strong and withstand those primitive and ancient forces. I whisper my mantra to myself.

"Remember the strawberries, remember the strawberries."

# OBSESSING ABOUT YARD WORK

The combination of children and yard work brings out the worst in me.

I blame my father for this.

His theory was that terrible things happen to boy children who do not perform yard work with enthusiasm. He had many stories about bad boys who didn't help their parents around the house and yard and he predicted miserable futures for these lazy, no good bums. They would never grow up to be Real Men (R.M.) able to survive in the Real World (R.W.). There were rules for Real Women (R.W.) in the R.W. also, but I won't go into those here. Suffice it to say one of the rules for R.W. was to make sure their sons turned into R.M. You can see what a burden I labored under.

Now I suspect my father was a little uptight about this R.M. stuff (to him doing dishes or eating vegetables meant you were not a R.M.) but nonetheless, I have been involuntarily imprinted with this picture of manhood.

So when weekends roll around, I feel it is imperative our sons be outside tilling the soil, routing out weeds, and subduing the lawn right next to their parents, with enthusiasm, preferably addressing us as "Sir" and "Ma'am."

I might add here that our whole yard is less than one fifth of an acre and our house sits right in the middle. But still, there are things to do.

It's always an uphill battle. Whenever we mention yard

work, we are greeted with stony silences and rolled eyes. When actually confronted with outdoor work, both sons immediately turn limp and weak. Rakes fall from their hands for no reason. They walk with the stoop of ninety-year-old men.

If they are required to throw weeds into a bag six inches away, the weeds clock in at about half the distance. And do they worry about getting out the roots? Never. A few upper leaves make the grade as far as they're concerned.

After years of futile screaming and yelling, I figured out that I was never going to get the enthusiasm I wanted about yard work and I might as well stop making a fool of myself. Besides, I'd been talking to other parents and found out our kids weren't the only work wimps. Most parents had given up trying.

The next time we were in the yard, I doled out jobs to the kids. They did them halfheartedly, but I kept my nose to the soil and tried not to look. I didn't call them names once. When they said they were finished, I thanked them and said they could go. (Boy, were they surprised!)

As I continued to work and sweat out in the sun, I could hear them inside the house, laughing and shooting rubber bands at each other. Despite my good intentions I felt irritated at the imperfectly weeded flower bed and the dirt left on the patio.

Finally I cracked. My father's rage boiled up in me. Those kids were getting away with murder, I thought.

I stomped around to the side yard where my husband was repairing the fence. He does not share my yard work obsessions, but then he didn't have the father I did. His father expected him to work hard, too hard he believed, and so he was trying to move in the other direction and be more lenient. This attitude really bugs me. I want to say, "Great! Your father turned you into a R.M. but you don't want to do the same for your own sons." But I keep these thoughts to myself. My husband looks at me oddly when I talk like this. He pretends he doesn't know what I'm talking about. Ha!

"Aren't you going to make the kids help you mix cement for the fence post?" I asked meaningfully.

"Oh, I wouldn't miss it," he said enigmatically.

"So then when, huh?"

"Oh, soon. Soon."

A few minutes later I heard him calling, "Oh boys, could you come out here? I need your advice and help on something."

At first I wanted to scream, but then I thought, hey, that's a good idea. Try flattery. Maybe it will work.

They tramped outside. After awhile I went over to see their progress. I saw them spooning dry cement into the post hole.

"Aren't you supposed to mix it with water first?" I asked.

"Well, the boys and I discussed it and we're trying something different," explained my husband.

"We're going to add water later," they told me, smiling and looking pleased with their brilliance.

I looked at them closely. They both appeared to have semi-alert looks on their faces. Their eyes were actually open all the way. They were working with some degree of urgency.

I could see that they were exhibiting qualities that even my father would describe as belonging to Real Men.

I felt my whole body relax.

It was going to be OK after all.

A few years later, when our sons were almost out of the nest and we had given up the yard work sessions simply because we were all too busy, my son Mark said in a reflective moment, "You know, in a perverse sort of way I miss all that yard work."

"You've got to be kidding. Why?"

"Well, it was the one time that we were really accomplishing something together as a family."

I assured him we could start again, but he said it was OK. He didn't miss it that much.

Which just goes to show you, parents don't have a clue as to what's really going on with their kids. You just have to hope that when they grow up they will tell you their side of the story.

# OUR BOY BILL

These are strange times. I can recall when the day's mail brought letters from people you actually knew.

Today, most of my mail is from organizations, many of which I didn't know existed, pleading and begging for money.

The same is true for phone calls. Used to be that people who called you up actually knew you, or at least knew your name.

But no longer; for more than a year we have been receiving phone calls, at the rate of twice a week or more, for a guy named Bill.

Now my husband's first initial is W. We figured his name got on a list somewhere, and some genius decided the W. stood for William, which it doesn't, which could then translate into "Bill."

All these phone calls have one thing in common. The caller is selling some oddball investment scheme such as drilling for oil in New York City or mining tin in the Ozarks, all guaranteed money makers too hot to pass up.

Perhaps the most annoying thing is that these people—always men—call Bill at home. Why they assume Bill lollygags at home all day I'll never know. But this means these would-be con artists are interrupting me or my sons in our lollygagging. We resent this.

When all this started, like fools, we politely explained

the whole mix-up about "W." and spent fifteen minutes listening to their spiels.

Then we began telling them up front we weren't interested in any investment-by-phone schemes. This cut the time down to ten minutes, for they were all determined to explain that they weren't selling anything.

Then we began telling them they had the wrong number.

But these people do not give up easily. Invariably, they inform me that they have it on good authority that this is indeed William's or Bill's phone number and it is I who am mistaken. Then they repeat the phone number for my edification.

Just today, a man called at 11 A.M. and asked if he had been able to "catch" Bill before he went to work.

Something inside me snapped. I'd had one too many interruptions. I hung up! The phone rang again. An angry voice said, "Don't you dare hang up on me." Click.

Now I'm out for revenge. My son Mark, who is also sick of being interrupted by phone calls for Bill, came up with a list of possible responses and the next time one of these jokers call, we hope to surprise him with one of the following:

"How did you get this number? This is the hot line between Moscow and Washington. You are jeopardizing national security. Hang up immediately. And incidentally, the CIA and FBI will be investigating you.

"Bill has changed his name to Maharishi. Would you like to speak with him? I'll see if he's out of his trance.

"What kind of insult is this? Are you insinuating my husband is a lazy bum sitting at home in the middle of the day? What is your name and whom do you represent?

"Bill hasn't spoken to anyone in over ten years and I don't think he'll change his ways for you. Besides, the last thing he said was, 'My name's not Bill.'

"He's in prison. Call back in twenty years.

"He's watching reruns of "Gilligan's Island" and has asked not to be disturbed.

"I'm sorry. Bill's out to lunch. (Organ Music). Permanently.

"I suppose you think you can pull a fast one, huh? Get Bill to invest the family savings in some harebrained scheme, and then run off with a twenty-year-old hussy and leave me and the children alone? I know how you guys work. I read the newspapers.

"The cat got his tongue. Bit it clear off. He's on antibiotics, not to mention in one heck of a lot of pain. Would you care to listen to his screams?

"Bill's a sandwich—ever since the roof fell on him.

"Congratulations! You have just won twelve free lessons at Bill's Dance Studio. Say the magic word and we'll throw in a toaster."

Or maybe we'll put the guy on hold and play "My Boy Bill" from Rodgers and Hammerstein's *Carousel*.

Excuse me, damnit. The phone's ringing.

# A SECRET MALE RITUAL

Men like to be perceived as mysterious beings. They hoard their trade secrets, handed down from their fathers, as if their lives depended on it.

However, I am pleased to report that by dint of incredible perseverance, I have penetrated one of their most zealously guarded secrets. And it only took me twenty years.

I'm talking about that uniquely male ritual of affixing objects—pictures, baskets and towel racks—onto walls.

For the first five years of our marriage, my husband managed to avoid what he called, "putting holes into innocent walls." But the birth of our second child and the purchase of a house wore him down. The inevitable occurred and it was time to install The First Towel Rack.

He went directly to a small wooden box which he'd kept concealed in the garage. Unlocking a secret combination, he opened the lid and pulled out a hand drill, a level, a hammer, a rusty coffee can filled with nails, and a tape measure, which he fastened to his belt loop. "I didn't know you came with a dowry," I said. He ignored me.

From his workbench, he picked up twelve screwdrivers and three hundred feet of extension cord and marched upstairs to the bathroom with a demeanor that suggested he was about to perform brain surgery on the President of the United States.

I followed at a discreet distance. For the first fifteen

minutes, the only thing he did was paw through the rusty can of nails, swear, and sigh.

"I hope your tetanus shot is up to date," I said.

He ignored me.

A trip to the store was required, since the towel rack had come with the wrong-sized screws and required an odd size. "Probably Japanese," he muttered as he ran down the stairs.

When he returned, he began rapping on the bathroom walls.

"Are you trying to make contact with someone?" I asked.

"I'm looking for 'studs,'" he said.

"Well, could you do that on your own time and put up the towel rack first?" I asked curtly.

"I'm looking for hardwood," he explained, in a tone suggesting this was something any idiot knew from birth.

"If I don't find hardwood," he continued, teeth clenched, "the towel rack will fall off the wall."

"What if there is no hardwood where we want the towel rack to go?"

A cloud passed over his face and he squinted at me.

"Then you have to use mollies. And mollies make very big holes in the wall."

I left him tapping and knocking. I suspected it was a delaying tactic to get me out of there. I'd asked one too many questions. He was afraid I might learn something.

After awhile the tapping and knocking died down, and I was summoned to the bathroom.

"Tell me exactly where you want the towel rack," he demanded.

"Uh, over there," I said, waving my hands in the approximate location.

"Are you sure? You do realize that I am going to be drilling holes in the wall, don't you?"

He held the now ominous looking chrome towel rack against the wall and demanded to know if it was level. When I hesitated, he informed me I'd better be sure or be prepared to live with it for the rest of my natural life. After all, he was going to be drilling holes in the wall.

By then, I was only too happy to leave the room while he performed his secret rituals. He emerged a while later, his clothes covered with white dust, and one towel rack affixed to the wall. "That sucker is there for eternity," he said proudly. "Oh, and by the way, vacuum up the dust, will you?"

Over the years curtain rods, more towel racks, and pictures got put up, but my role continued to be standing around, occasionally fetching a Phillips screwdriver or a yardstick, and sweeping up.

The secrecy continued. He used words like toggle bolts, ⁵⁄₃₂s and expansion anchors. When I asked him how he knew these things he said, "Everybody knows these things," or "I just know."

Eventually, my ability to purchase objects to put up on the walls outstripped my husband's willingness to mount them. Our house became littered with pictures, baskets, certificates, photographs, and metal organizational systems, all leaning against the walls, unable to make the great leap upwards.

I began fantasizing about doing the job myself, but all the talk of drill bits and levels had done its work. I was intimidated.

Besides, my husband had trained our sons to watch me. If they sensed any movement toward making a hole in the wall, they'd say, "Shouldn't you check with Dad first?"

Finally, I got fed up. I'd had two baskets sitting on my dresser since a year ago last summer, waiting for my husband. It was obvious either I would mount them on the wall or they would rot.

I marched out to the garage and looked at the rat's nest my husband calls a workbench. I yanked open every one of the two hundred plastic drawers. In the last one I spotted a cunning little bag of gold hooks which had been bought years ago to install cups under the cabinet. The cups are still stacked five high inside the kitchen cupboard, but the hooks were in my hand. I went into the house.

"I'm going to go upstairs and put holes in the walls," I taunted my husband.

He claimed he couldn't hear me over the baseball game.

"You're in denial," I told him and repeated my communiqué. He turned up the TV.

Upstairs, I faced The Wall. I looked at the hook. It had a little threaded end. Questions raced through my mind: Would I have to find a stud? Would I need mollies?

I knocked on the walls for awhile, but wasn't sure what I was listening for. I hoped a little voice would say, "Here, put the screw in here."

Finally my mind said, "Just do it."

I had just pressed the screw to the wall when my son's hulking shadow blocked the light.

"What are you doing?" he asked, trying to sound casual.

"I'm actually going to put something up on the walls. I'm forty-two years old. I think it's time, don't you?"

"You'd better check with Dad," he said.

I glared at him defiantly as I twisted the little hook into the wall. The plasterboard gave way nicely and I had a hook on which to place one basket.

I hung it up.

"It will probably fall down," he said.

We watched in silence. It showed no signs of falling down. I purposefully picked up a second hook. Defeated, my son left, while I put up the second basket.

It was so easy I couldn't believe it. I looked at my little

bag of gold hooks. What power! With these sweeties, I could mount anything under five pounds that I wanted. There was no limit to the number of holes I could punch in the walls.

So this was the secret power men have been trying to keep for themselves. I laughed out loud. A delicious sense of freedom washed over me as images of myself confidently using drills and mollies and nails whirled before my eyes.

At long last! The walls are mine!

# ON
# THE
# ROAD

# YOU CAN'T GO AWAY AGAIN

Once upon a time we packed up the stroller, the Pampers, and the plastic sand buckets and took our two sons to San Diego, a place of warm breezes, blue ocean, and the largest zoo in the world.

Ten years later we had the bright idea to retrace that path and take our sons back to where they'd had such a wonderful time. Some of our favorite photographs show them in overalls and red baseball caps toddling around the San Diego Zoo, delighted with the pink flamingos and giraffes, and feeding peanuts to the squirrels.

We had an inkling this trip would be different when the 11-year-old blurted out he didn't want to go. He'd just graduated from sixth grade, leaving a close knit group of buddies. He was afraid of missing a hot game of Dungeons and Dragons over in Lenny's garage.

"Oh but you'll love the zoo, the aquarium, and the ride down the coast," we told him.

He dutifully threw his clothes in the suitcase and seemed resigned to endure a week with his family.

The 13-year-old wasn't any better. He packed without whining, but insisted on taking a Dramamine before setting foot into the car and fell asleep before we got out of town. We didn't hear from him until the second day when he woke up as we stopped at an art gallery and crafts shop along the coast highway.

"Are we in San Diego?" he asked. When we said no, he demanded to know what we thought we were "accomplishing" by stopping at crafts shops.

Life can be so cruel. After I had finally convinced my husband it was "fun" to stop along the way, my son adopts the ancient male point of view that says the whole point of any trip is getting to the destination ASAP.

He continued to ask when we would "arrive" in San Diego. As soon as we arrived, he began asking when we were going to go home.

"Why are you so anxious to be home?" I asked. "You're going to be there the rest of the summer."

He lowered his eyelids, gazed toward the horizon, and replied cryptically that he "had things to do."

It was an odd trip in many ways. The Santa Ana winds were blowing and the air felt like it was blasting out of a giant furnace. Fires blazed on the surrounding mountains. Rumor had it that cars might be stopped and men forced to help fight the flames.

Everywhere we went, our sons followed at a distance. "Oh look at the flamingos," we pointed out while walking at the zoo. "Oh how you loved them." They looked at us darkly and muttered between themselves. It was hard to imagine those two precious toddlers had grown into these brooding hulks.

On our last day, we got up early for the twelve-hour drive home. At breakfast, we asked our sons what part of the trip they liked best.

"Right before we left home," said the 13-year-old.

Being stupid, or maybe desperate for a shred of gratitude, we asked what their favorite meal had been. Was it the charming Mexican restaurant where we ate out on a garden patio? Or the lunch overlooking the Pacific?

No, it was the dinner from the convenience store—hot

dogs, soda, and chocolate cupcakes—they'd eaten in front of the TV the night my husband and I had gone out to celebrate our sixteenth wedding anniversary.

But the cruelest cut of all came the following morning when we were back at home. The phone rang. It was Lenny, calling to see how the trip had been.

"It was terrible," we heard the 11-year-old say.

"No one was there."

# LURCHING THROUGH
# THE CAPITAL

One summer my sons and I took a trip to the nation's capital. My husband stayed home, recovering from a back injury, while I forged ahead on the educational tour to star in the role of SuperMom. My sons must have sensed my intention, for they challenged and thwarted me at every turn.

"Where are we leaving from?" they asked as soon as I announced my plans. When I said San Jose instead of the usual San Francisco, they squinted their teenaged eyes at me and asked if I were "sure" planes went to Washington, D.C. from San Jose.

At the airline check-in desk my sons announced to the agent, "We want window seats."

"The plane is very full," the agent replied, raising his eyebrows and peering at us over his glasses. "Did you reserve your seats when you made your reservations?"

"Uh, no," I admitted. I hadn't known you could do that. My sons gave me a look that would wither a zucchini plant.

By the time the agent finished scratching his head and consulting his computer, I was grateful for three seats anywhere, as long as they were on the plane.

"You won't be sitting together," he warned. I smiled bravely and said that was all right.

We boarded the plane and found our seats. Mine was next to a handsome man who, when he realized my son was in another aisle, offered to switch seats. I said that wouldn't be necessary and talked to him non-stop, knowing it would be the last time I spoke to another adult for a week. As I chatted, I struggled to ignore the pitiful looks my younger son was broadcasting to me from his spot in the front row, where he was forced to sit with his backpack on his lap. Later, he told me he'd been sandwiched between a lady who did not speak English but kept trying to practice on him, and a chubby kid who overflowed his seat and wiggled all the time. And he held me responsible for these transgressions against his person.

We landed at National Airport, climbed into a cab and soon discovered that the D.C. taxi drivers are devotees of the Kamikaze School of Driving. Our lunatic, excuse me, driver sped in and out of spaces the size of shoe boxes. I gripped the seat and cursed myself for subjecting my sons to certain death or grievous injury. I glanced at them to offer comfort, but they were grinning broadly.

"Hey, this is fun," one said, as we spurted around a corner and almost skidded up onto the lawn of the National Gallery of Art.

By a stroke of incredible luck, we arrived safely at our hotel. The desk clerk told us apologetically that my room did not adjoin the boys'. They would be down the hall.

I smiled bravely and said that was all right. I sensed the boys giving each other high fives behind my back.

No sooner had I sat down to recover when they rushed into my room waving glossy brochures.

"Guess what? The hotel has HBO. They show movies. For free. All the time." My heart sank as I wondered if I would ever get them out of the hotel.

After dinner I mentioned the National Symphony would be playing on the west lawn of the Capitol. They told me *Mommy Dearest* would be on TV in five minutes.

Over at the beautifully lighted Capitol, the symphony

played a wonderful collection of music celebrating America: music from *Annie* and a medley of folk songs and hoedown tunes. Unfortunately, for me, the music was accompanied by the staccato moanings of my son who insisted he had to go to the bathroom right that minute or else he would die.

The next evening I left one of my charges at the hotel to watch a James Bond movie and took my older son out to the Tidal Basin. We rented a paddle boat and pumped over to the Jefferson Memorial where the Army Band was giving a concert.

We got as close as we dared, heeding the posted signs warning of sharp rocks. It took exactly three measures of "Surrey with the Fringe on Top" for my son to decide he hated the music. "Let's go back," he said.

I told him I hadn't pumped all the way out there for nothing and we were staying.

He retaliated by developing a case of major hiccups. Soon the reverberations were skimming over the water and bouncing off the walls of the Memorial. I thought they might have to cancel the concert. Or worse, I could imagine the force tipping us over, impaling us on sharp rocks, our screams drowned out by the strains of, "Some Enchanted Evening."

When I couldn't stand it any longer, we returned to the shore. I treated my son to two of my East Coast childhood favorites unavailable at home—Orange Crush soda and Wise Potato Chips. While we waited for the taxi, my son informed me he didn't "feel well" and then proceeded to throw up on the lawn around the Tidal Basin to the shock of the couples necking in the balmy summer evening.

The next morning we joined a very long line of people waiting to tour the FBI Building. The sign told us it would take an hour. To ward off heat prostration, I sent one son off for sodas. Immediately, the line moved and we were ready to go in. As the guard searched my purse for God knows what, I confessed one member of our party was at the McDonald's across the street. He told us to get back in line.

Eventually we got in and, as we listened to a young agent tell us about the FBI's investigative techniques, my son leaned toward me and asked if he could borrow my mirror. His contact lens had "slipped off his eyeball."

Unfortunately, in a small attempt to lighten my purse that morning, I had taken out my mirror.

While we whispered things like, "Push it back on," and "I can't," and, "Move your eyeball under it," and "I can't," the guide told us fingerprints are the only conclusive means of identification and a murder is committed every twenty-three minutes in the United States. Yes, I wondered briefly, but how often in the FBI Building?

When the guide paused and asked if there were any questions, I raised my hand and said, "Does anyone have a mirror?" All the women began pawing through their purses and my son told me I was embarrassing him.

As fate would have it, as soon as we had a mirror, the lens popped out onto the floor as the entire crowd watched. Another agent was summoned to personally escort my son to the bathroom where he could reinsert his lens. He missed the part about becoming an FBI agent. I think the Bureau would be grateful to know that I didn't fill him in.

And so the trip continued. The next day, after fifteen minutes in the History Wing of the Smithsonian, my sons told me they'd "seen everything" and were ready to return to the hotel. Later, in Georgetown, they told me there was "nothing to do."

At the end of the trip we visited with relatives. When my traveling companions were asked what they had seen or done in the nation's capital, they summed up the whole experience in two words.

"Nothing much."

My failure as traveling SuperMom was exposed. Upon later reflection, I realized I was lucky. At least they didn't blow my cover completely and mention their midnight viewings in their hotel room of *Mommy Dearest* and *The Best Little Whorehouse in Texas.*

It's funny. I turned forty on that trip. And to think, I'd only been thirty-five when we left home.

# CHEWING OUR WAY
## ACROSS EUROPE

Before I left home for a trip to Europe with my family, I bid au revoir to my kitchen. I had cooked my Last Supper (Medley of Leftovers). "Out of the kitchen and onto the Continent," I shouted, twirling my dishrag.

I imagined myself sipping café au lait at outdoor tables along the Champs-Élysées, quaffing warm beer and bangers in wood-panelled English pubs, and being served dishes with exotic names in establishments featuring white table-cloths and at least two forks.

I forgot I was going to be accompanied by two teenagers with over-developed mouth muscles and hollow bodies. "When do we eat?" became the rallying cry at each and every stop.

On our first evening in Paris, we strolled along the Champs-Élysées. Our companions insisted they were "starving." We entered a cafe at 6 P.M., a good two hours before any self-respecting French restaurant serves dinner. All the Parisians were sipping drinks at the outside tables while we were herded into a back room where the waiter told us we could order a jambon sandweech (a ham sandwich), a from-age sandweech (a cheese sandwich), or a jambon et fromage sandweech. Just what we chose escapes me now, but I keenly remember feeling aced out of the total Paris experience.

The next day, back on the Champs, the gang spied a

Burger King and insisted they needed fortification before scaling the Arc de Triomphe.

"Let's just finish the tour and then we'll find a picturesque restaurant," I said.

"It takes too long to find picturesque," they wailed. "We're hungry now." With the two of them bleating in unison, we capitulated.

Inside, my son used some of his money to buy a T-shirt that said "Burger King—Paris."

There was one touch of elegance. A fellow in a tuxedo and slicked-back hair prowled around and told people to keep their feet off the chairs and not to mess with the ketchup.

At the Eiffel Tower, the galloping gourmands discovered a quickie restaurant were you could order Chicken and French fries, or French fries and Chicken. We ate there. My husband said the whining was wearing him down and he didn't care any more.

We never made it for éclairs and café au lait on Place Madeleine. We did, however, purchase ice cream cones from every single street vendor in Paris.

At the Louvre, our two trash compactors on legs dragged around as though they had cement in their Adidas. But they perked up when they noticed a snack area.

"You ate breakfast only an hour ago," my husband reminded them.

"But we're starving now."

"Well I think you can go a little longer without an intravenous feeding," he hissed.

The rest of that museum tour was pas de jolly.

But that didn't stop them for long. As we drove toward the Loire Valley, we dined at a roadside restaurant where our oldest son ordered two dinners and asked for a third. When we suggested he nibble some of the chocolate he'd purchased in Amsterdam, he confessed he'd eaten all five pounds the day he bought it, in a desperate attempt to ward off starvation.

We also feasted at the lunch bar at the Charles de Gaulle Airport in preparation for the grueling one-hour flight over the English Channel.

At the Tower of London, we toured the chapel where Anne Boleyn and Lady Jane Grey were entombed and heard the grisly details of English beheading habits. As we emerged, shaken, from the dark chapel into the sunlight, my son said, "Is anyone else as hungry as I am?"

While my stomach and mind reeled from the possibility that food might be served within ten miles of the Tower of London, they located The Tower of London Snack Shoppe and Eatery. We ate at the outdoor picnic benches while black ravens the size of cats prowled around our feet for crumbs or heaven knows what else.

"We need a little something to tide us over before we see the Chamber of Horrors," our sons said at Madame Tussaud's Wax Museum.

As I shivered in the icy air of the lunchroom, adjusted for the comfort of the wax figures placed tastefully about, I watched my sons put away English pies featuring lumps of mystery meat floating in a grey sauce, and wondered how it was that I had come to this place at this time, with these strange people.

Later, as we drove down to Canterbury, the kids looked meaningfully at every "Tea and Snacks" shack we passed. We ignored them.

When we stopped to change drivers, they came alert. "Are we going to eat?" they asked.

"No!" I shouted.

"I sure hope they have restaurants in Canterbury," said one son. He didn't have to worry. As we drove into town, a

Big Mac wrapper flew up onto the hood of the car. Indeed, on the very same cobblestones where pilgrims trod centuries ago, modern pilgrims can grab a box of Kentucky Fried Chicken, a cheeseburger at McDonald's, or a pizza at Pizza Hut.

Our sons insisted on buying lots of snacks for the eleven-hour flight back to San Francisco. "They only serve two meals," they explained, claiming they would "die" on that regimen.

At home, they said they'd barely survived the trip, they felt emaciated, and their clothes were too loose. One son told me he'd lost ten pounds.

As for me, I gained ten pounds just being with them.

So now, it's tuna and celery sticks for me. I wouldn't mind if those pounds consisted of croissants or éclairs or café au lait.

But burgers and ham sandwiches?

Oh puhleeze . . .

# CAREENING ALONG
# THE COUNTRYSIDE

Figures released by the travel industry indicate a shockingly high incidence of divorce among American couples who travel abroad. The most significant contributing factor appears to be driving. Of all American couples who rent a car in Europe, a full 51 percent agree to get divorced on the spot. Of those remaining, one third will separate within a month. The remainder resort to episodes of vicious fighting and name-calling that can last a lifetime.

On a family trip to Europe, my husband and I decided to rent a car after touring Paris. We planned to leave the city and "see the countryside."

On the appointed day, we rose early, left our children at the hotel, and took the subway to the Hertz Rental office.

"Zahr ees no gas in zee automobile," the rental agent said apologetically, as he handed us the keys to a faded blue Ford Sierra.

"Could you direct us to the nearest gas station?" my husband asked calmly.

"Eet ees veddy deefeecult, because all zee streets are zee one way."

"Could you show us on the map?" asked my husband, now only pretending to be calm.

Fear clutched my insides as I realized that I would be expected to read and understand that map.

My map-reading skills had been severely stunted in the

fourth grade, when I read the complete set of Nancy Drew mysteries during geography class. The minute the teacher pulled down the map and began pointing out rivers, tributaries, and mountain ranges, I caught up with the supersleuth from the book concealed in my lap.

My skills at map reading were further thwarted when I married a map genius who can find an itty bitty spot on a map and figure out how to get there while driving at 80 miles an hour.

So it's his fault I haven't had any practice.

A few minutes later, saddled with a map written in a foreign language, a car with no gas, and an irritable maniac at the wheel, we pull out into Paris traffic. The car stalls. Drivers honk but go around us like water around a stone.

We lurch further out into the traffic. More honking.

"Get the map," my husband growls.

I stare wistfully at a church and ask for guidance as we jerk by.

Craning my neck out the window, I search for street signs, which are thoughtlessly placed high up on the buildings, with no care given for tourists driving economy-sized cars.

Streets begin and end with no warning; a maze of unnamed side streets radiate from every intersection. This is too much even for the map genius.

We can't figure out where the traffic lights are, but it doesn't really make any difference because the cross-traffic is always blocking the intersection. The only way to get through is to edge the stalling, lurching car into the phalanx of other cars until some driver is forced to let us through. But they don't acquiesce without protest.

The car continues to stall. Suddenly, a van delivering l'eau minerale stops ahead on a one-way street filled with five snaking lanes of traffic, and the driver leaps out to make a delivery.

"A lesser person would just leave this car in the middle of the street, lock the keys inside, and stroll quietly away," says my husband. This sounds like a good idea, but I don't want to admit to being a "lesser person."

By driving in ever widening circles we reach a gas station where a wonderful man puts gas in the car. I resist the urge to kiss his hands. We begin our complicated weaving back to our hotel. We find our two sons have begun preparing to live as orphans.

Weaving out of Paris toward Versailles, we find ourselves on one-way streets that go in circles. The car stalls every five minutes. The only sound in the car is that of my index finger tracing our route on the map. I don't dare lift it. I did for a second to scratch my head and my husband accused me of "not taking the situation seriously enough."

At the town of Versailles, we find a Hertz office and exchange our balky blue Ford for a sleek green Peugeot with a sun roof, electric windows, and a silky non-stalling engine. At the Palace we're so happy we grin and mug in front of the Hall of Mirrors.

As we tool toward the Loire Valley on a road that looks like a freeway, I lift my now arthritic index finger from the map and offer to drive.

"Are you prepared to go 80 miles an hour?" snaps my husband. "Because that's what they are driving here."

"Are you calling me a sissy just because I stick to the speed limit at home? Well I'm not spineless. Pull over, Buster."

I adjust the sun roof, get a quick review on shifting in five gears, and floor it.

The teenagers actually wake up. "Hey, way to go Mom," they shout. I give my husband a triumphant glance. He's turned white.

Soon I am doing 90, or so my husband says, his voice

shaking. I can't tell. The car is smooth and the speedometer is marked in kilowatts or something.

"Wanna try for 100?" I say, laughing hysterically.

"No, no," whimpers my husband. I tell him to relax. He tells me it's impossible. As we get off onto small country roads, the silence is punctuated with remarks like, "Do you realize how close you are to the side of the road?" and "You almost hit the Renault." And when it takes me twenty tries to find reverse, while perched on a steep hill in the shadow of a cathedral, my husband asks in an insinuating tone, "Do you want me to drive?"

Somehow we survive France. Our next stop is London where, forgetting our past, we rent a car and head out of town.

For the first hour all the other drivers honk and gesture at us. Before our nerves are completely shot, we discover they're telling us part of a seatbelt is hanging out the door.

At least here the roads are well marked and the map is in the right language. But you have to drive on the wrong side of the road with a steering wheel on the wrong side of the car.

Out of the city, I gallantly offer to drive. I creep out onto the road repeating to myself, "Left, left, left." Again my husband asks if I "realize" how close I am to the side of the road. I can't help it; I'm trying to stay out of the oncoming traffic. My instincts tell me I'm safer driving in the fields.

"Hey look," yells one son. "The sheep are starting to act nervous." I want to give him a dirty look but I don't dare turn around.

Finally I start to feel comfortable.

"Hey I'm doing it! I've never driven in England before."

"Oh yes you have," says my husband. "It was when we were here sixteen years ago. I'll never forget it. You almost clipped a milkman. I was never so frightened in my whole life. And I'll never forget the look on the milkman's face, either."

I threaten to never speak to him again. He reminds me I also say mean things while he drives, such as when I suggest that the pedestrians crossing the street might want to live to see their next birthdays.

Fortunately it's soon time to go home.

Just in time to avoid a messy divorce.

# Seasons
# and
# Celebrations

# THE HIGH ANXIETY SEASON

As the days wind down toward the last day of school, my anxiety level is rising. While the words, "summer vacation" are so exciting to children, they cause palpitations in adults who will have to be with their children full-time for the, uh, er, entire summer.

I pretend to share my children's excitement about the upcoming school vacation and their plans to "just lie around and relax." But inside I'm seething because I know if a kid isn't at school, he's, well, at home.

And if there's one thing that drives us red-blooded mothers crazy, it's watching junior lie around and relax all day every day. Especially when we feel overworked and frazzled, trying to maintain our own activities while attempting to pin down and coordinate the unfolding schedules of the layabout generation.

There is a solution. And that is to get the kid out of the house. But have you ever noticed how much time and money it takes to actually eject a kid from the house for any length of time? It's the equivalent of a part-time job to supervise the effort.

Summer school is the obvious solution but unless your child is very young or very naive, it is impossible to foist upon them a schedule of word problems and book reports. They're American children, they will tell you, and they are fully entitled under the Bill of Rights to have a summer vacation. They will also tell you it's a medical necessity. They need to "rest their brains."

There is, of course, the camp alternative. But these days, a kid needs a fully formed identity before a selection can be made. Will it be music camp, soccer camp, horsebackriding camp, backpacking camp, or will the kid get a leg up on his career and attend computer camp? The choices give me a headache. In my day you went to Girl Scout or Boy Scout Camp and learned how to swim in a cold lake with icky fish in it, to burn hotdogs on a pointy stick, weave lanyards, and learn how to sing "Ninety-Nine Bottles of Beer on the Wall." That was about it. Today, I'm afraid all these specialty camps will forge irrevocable changes in my children's lives instead of simply providing a place to fool around outdoors, away from home.

Our children did go to camp for a few summers. Our oldest chose Camp New Horizons, which focused on "the development of the whole person within the natural environment."

Not only was this camp expensive, it required a full week of shopping to acquire the correct gear: leather hiking boots, custom backpacking frame, a duffel bag with a side zipper, and one hundred percent cotton socks. The last two items were not available anywhere in the Free World or at least nowhere near my house.

This week of shopping was then topped off by a hot, five-hour drive to the Sierra where this camp was located.

As they got older, they refused to go to camp, preferring to stay home and nickel and dime me to death. They waited until I became unhinged and was attacking the grout in the kitchen counters with toothpicks before they'd say, "Can we go to the movies? And, by the way, we have no money."

By then, $10 for three hours of peace and quiet seemed like a bargain.

One summer I considered sending them back to visit relatives on the East Coast. But this evoked a mild panic in me as I looked at our California kids through the eyes of our kin. I saw boys with holes in their sneakers, wearing mismatched socks, sporting longish locks and occasionally, in moments of passion, letting loose with a no-good, very-bad word or two. No, I couldn't subject our relatives, or myself, to that.

Another summer I decided to teach them how to ride the county buses. I tacked the bus route map on the refrigerator and pointed out places of interest—movie theaters, shopping malls and zoos in far away cities, plus their father's place of employment. As I stood at various bus stops seeing them off, I comforted myself with the thought that once they learned the secrets of the transit system, they'd insist on taking long trips away from home.

Alas, it did not work. They hated the buses. They were afraid of getting lost. And they insisted they saw "weird people" on the bus.

"Stay home one more hour and you'll see weird right in your very own home," I grumbled.

Aside from camp, long bus trips, or visits to relatives, there are music lessons, drama lessons, art lessons, and swimming lessons, all to be driven to in a car (preferably air conditioned) by Mommy.

There's no doubt about it; summer is no picnic for mothers. I remember one July morning walking into my bedroom, looking into the mirror, sobbing quietly and wondering if I would be able to hold on until September.

My biggest problem is that I'm the kind of person who desperately wants to have things orderly and to have the world make sense, and with two boys close in age, who are experts at arguing and insulting each other about every single thing, some days nothing seemed to make sense.

So here I am, heart palpitating, pulse racing, as my precious days of freedom run out and my children's vacation looms.

I'm really worried this year. Nothing is scheduled. And our kids are too old to sign them up for anything against their will.

There is one glimmer of hope: my older son might possibly get his driver's license this summer. Maybe he'd like to run an errand for me? Like in Los Angeles?

"And take your brother with you!" I'll scream.

I don't know. There's the other problem too.

I always miss them when they're gone.

# TUXEDO TRAUMA

June—the season of the Great Tuxedo Renting Ritual; a feat which takes almost as much effort as getting into college.

The good news is that unless you live with a prospective groom or prom attendee, you can avoid this nervewracking ritual. The bad news is that a need for a tuxedo can present itself without warning.

It happened to me when my sophomore son came home and announced that a junior girl had invited him to the Junior Prom. And the prom was less than a week away.

I quickly sent out a call to my network. Did anyone have a tuxedo lurking in a closet? My sources turned up one orange tuxedo jacket purchased for $1 at a garage sale. I didn't even suggest this option to my son. He's bigger than I am and I try to avoid irritating him.

Next, we called our nearest tuxedo supplier to ask how far in advance we had to place our order. "Come in immediately," the clerk said. "Or else it will be too late."

We ran to the car and started driving.

On the way, my son told me he was surprised to learn his father had only worn a tuxedo once.

I wasn't surprised. I remember the time well. It was at our wedding. Ten minutes before the ceremony, my husband-to-be discovered the rented trousers were three sizes too small. To this day he insists he remembers nothing of the wedding because his mind was fully occupied willing his pants not to split apart in front of three hundred people.

At the store we joined a long line of guys who looked like football players and wrestlers meekly choosing baby pink and powder blue cummerbunds and hankies to match their dates' dresses.

While we waited, my son leafed through a book of jacket styles: traditional, contemporary, double-breasted, or tails, available in white, black, gray, purple, or pin stripe. The choices were staggering.

"I know I don't want tails," he said emphatically and settled on a double-breasted style in gray.

I was so relieved one of us knew what we were doing that the $59 price tag didn't bother me at all.

Later I discovered that the $59 did not include the pleated shirt with wing collar, cummerbund (light blue), matching hanky, bow tie, and de rigueur white patent leather shoes.

The salesman measured him quickly by flicking a tape measure in the air around him and told us to return on Saturday.

The day of the prom we waited in a line of assorted males, only to discover that what was attached to a hanger with my son's name on it was an aging, white tuxedo jacket with soiled edges, undoubtedly from years of being fingered by nervous sophomores and uneasy grooms.

We appealed to the manager, who assured us he was sorry but the warehouse was fresh out of double-breasted jackets.

"We do have white tails, though, brand new, just your size," he told my son who seemed to be deflating in front of me. "Someone was supposed to pick them up, but if you want them, they're yours."

I opened my mouth to say, "The one thing he doesn't

want are tails," when my son piped up. "I thought it over; tails are OK."

He slipped on the jacket. The word "penguin" leaped to my mind, but I kept my mouth shut.

"Is anyone else wearing tails?" I asked discreetly.

He told me he didn't know.

"Don't you at least want to look in the mirror?"

"No, Mom," he said, exasperated. "And be quiet. I know everybody here." This latter surprised me because no one was talking to anybody else.

That evening, while he dressed, I kept an eye on the front walk in case the guy who ordered the tails in the first place came over to reclaim them. The rest of me worried how my conservative son, who once told me a gray striped shirt was "too loud to wear in public" would handle it if he turned out to be the only guy in tails at the whole prom. Would he end up scarred for life like his father, never able to wear a tuxedo again? Would I have another tuxedo casualty on my hands?

His date arrived to pick him up. (As a younger man, he didn't yet have his driver's license.) As I watched him climb into the car wearing his white tails, I feared the worst.

The next day, I searched his face for signs of trauma. None were apparent.

"How was the dance?" I asked casually.

"Fun," he said calmly.

"How were the tails?" I asked extra casually.

"Fine," he said. "There were three other people wearing tails."

Whew! I relaxed for the first time in twenty-four hours. Tuxedo Trauma had been staved off at our house, for now anyway.

Maybe it will skip a generation.

Or maybe it had already claimed its victim—me.

# CONFESSIONS OF A CANDY POACHER

I've been carrying the burden far too long. My therapist tells me I should deal with my guilt. My lawyer says no jury would convict me. My kids have come to think of it as "normal." After all, I'm the only mother they have.

My secret?

For years, I stole, that's right—filched, snatched, purloined, grabbed—Halloween candy. From my very own children.

But that's all behind me now. I've been rehabilitated.

How?

Simple. The kids are too old to go trick-or-treating, so there isn't any candy to steal.

My habit began years ago. I watched my two little boys, one dressed as Casper the Friendly Ghost and the other as Snoopy, come home from trick-or-treating dragging full, lumpy pillowcases.

They gleefully dumped their loot onto the floor, tossing out anything nutritious like apples or raisins and counting and sorting the rest, while gobbling up all the miniature Hershey Bars.

Did they offer me anything? Never. If I begged, they'd part with a nougat or a stale caramel, tops. I could never pry a Three Musketeers or a bag of M & M's out of their greedy little fists.

"Go out and get your own," they'd tell me. "We walked ten miles to get this stuff."

As they grew older, they went trick-or-treating with plastic garbage bags, and pounded the pavement until they were filled.

It reached a point where they raked in so much loot, they were unable to consume their take in one sitting on Halloween night.

The upshot of this was that once they were in school, I was alone in the house with The Bags.

I remember the first time. I opened the door to my son's room. He was such an innocent—his bag was in full view on his bed.

To escape detection, I only took small candies like Mary Janes or Tootsie Rolls. First I'd go in one's room, then the other's. I probably made twenty trips a day in and out. If they ever wondered why I kept having to go to the dentist to get my teeth glued back on they never let on.

After awhile, however, they began to notice candy wrappers in unauthorized locations, such as falling out of my pockets.

They took immediate steps to halt the candy drain. First they tried to train the dog to guard their rooms. I solved that problem by sharing. Our dog is wild for Almond Joys.

Next, they took to recording their stock in notebooks in pen and counting it as soon as they arrived home from school. A little Liquid Paper did the trick there.

They resorted to hiding their candy. One year I had to fish my treats out of the laundry hamper; another year, from a trumpet case.

As they got older, they began to play dirty.

They put the candy in their desk drawers, locked them, and wore the keys on chains around their necks.

Now I have prided myself on being a mother who would

never invade her children's privacy by searching through their drawers, especially locked ones. Only the most extreme of circumstances forced me to suspend my code of ethics for the first two weeks in November. But let me just say, picking a lock with a Bic pen can take forever.

Then one day, something almost stopped me. It was a rainy November day. I was trying to write an article and it wasn't going well. I heard a Sugar Daddy calling my name.

I got up and went into my younger son's room. The voice was coming from the nightstand. I yanked the drawer open. At first I was amazed to see all the candy laid out in even rows, sorted as to type: chocolate bars arranged by brands, lollipops, bubblegum, little cellophane bags of candy corn, and so on. I had no idea he had such extensive organizational skills.

Then I noticed a piece of paper. It was a note addressed to me.

"Dear Mom, This drawer contains all of my meager Halloween candy collection. Please don't."

It was signed simply, Mark.

That note almost stopped me from filching a piece of candy. But not quite.

As I marvelled that he knew the word "meager," I located my Sugar Daddy and returned to typing and periodically prying the Sugar Daddy off my teeth.

The next day I went to the dentist's office to get my bridge cemented back on.

The Halloween poaching continued until the miserable day when they claimed they were "too old" to go out.

I tried to encourage them. I offered to make them elaborate costumes. At fifteen and sixteen they were, "above going out dressed as R2D2 and E.T. and hitting up the neighbors for candy."

"But how will I get any Halloween candy?" I whined.

"Just go to the store and buy some," they told me.

I tried that. But candy never tastes as good as when it's stolen from a small boy's cache.

As part of my act of confession, I asked my son what he thought of the fact that his mother used to steal his candy. He said it was about what he expected from me. He added piously that he would never steal candy from his children.

"I'd ask them politely, and if they said no, I'd accept it," he said.

"And then I'd punch their lights out," he added with a grin.

# DON'T EXPECT ME TO TALK TURKEY

Come November, images of turkeys begin to invade my consciousness, and no it's not because of the elections. These images increase as Thanksgiving draws closer, cropping up occasionally in my nightmares as I dream I have to stuff and truss a hundred-pound bird all by myself.

While I have no personal grudge against turkeys, I do have mixed feelings: Love to eat, hate to cook.

To be precise, it's not the cooking of the turkey that offends me, but rather the pressing of the flesh that I can't stand. The actual putting of one's hands on something which has so obviously had its head chopped off is not only frightening, but a trifle ghoulish to this middle-aged sissy.

As if the head business isn't bad enough, I'll never forget the day I discovered that the turkey manufacturers have the impudence and bad manners to put the neck and other unmentionables back into the turkey for us unsuspecting women to discover.

For years, this grisly custom was unknown to me; every Thanksgiving while I bustled around the kitchen, making fruit salad and gravy, my husband did the dirty work of preparing the turkey for the oven.

What he did with those nails and string, I didn't ask. I occupied myself cutting up symmetrical cubes of white bread with the electric carving knife, pretending nothing ghastly was happening right on my own kitchen counters.

My disenchantment came when I decided to cook a turkey on a day that wasn't Thanksgiving—a day when my husband was at work and my children at school.

After defrosting the bird in the refrigerator for the required number of days (I take what the package says and multiply by three), I boldly lifted the squishy mass onto the counter.

I began to get queasy as I struggled to spring the bird from its wrappings, stabbing the tough plastic covering with a butcher knife. (I had a surrealistic vision of myself as an actress in an Alfred Hitchcock film.)

Finally, the covering yielded up a turkey, and I barely got the whole mess to the sink before a strange red liquid (was that blood?) began to seep out.

It was downhill from there. The instructions in my *Fanny Farmer Cookbook* said to "lightly stuff the neck cavity." Egads. I didn't know where the neck cavity was, and didn't want to find out. Then I got a grip on myself and realized it had to be at the opposite end from the legs.

Bravely pulling up the flap of skin, using eight layers of paper towels while gazing steadfastly at the ceiling, I lightly stuffed the general area.

As I went on to stuff the body cavity, I discovered to my horror that there was something already in there.

I called my husband at work. "There's something in the turkey," I whispered. "What is it?"

He broke it to me slowly: "It's the neck and giblets. They put them in the bird."

"Why?" I screamed, suddenly afraid to be home alone with a turkey neck and giblets. Whatever giblets were, it didn't sound good.

"Some people cook them and cut the meat up for gravy or stuffing," he explained, lying through his teeth.

I knew that couldn't be the real reason, but I didn't have the stamina to argue.

I returned to the scene of the crime. I wanted to quit, but having already cut up twelve cups of bread cubes wedded me to the task.

But how to get the neck out? I first tried dumping it out, by holding the turkey up and shaking. But of course that would have been too easy. Next, I reached for my long-handled tongs. Inserting this implement into the bird, which was now reminding me more and more of a corpse, I felt the tongs close onto the cartilage rings of the neck.

I immediately dropped the tongs and danced around the kitchen in a little circle, chanting, "Ugh! Ick! Ugh!"

I considered calling on my children for help, but I was afraid of what the school principal would think if a child were summoned home early to help his mother pull the neck out of a turkey.

Tongs in hand, I tried valiantly to wrest the neck from its moorings. After each pull, I repeated my little chant and dance around the kitchen.

Finally, by late afternoon, the neck and innards dropped into a waiting pail, which I immediately delivered outside to the garbage cans.

Ignoring the rest of the instructions, especially the part about the nails, I tied the legs together tightly and shoved the poor thing into the oven.

I don't recall if I actually ate any of that particular turkey. I probably spent the entire evening lying in bed with a cold compress on my forehead. But I had learned a valuable lesson: Never again would I tempt the gods and cook a turkey on a day other than Thanksgiving.

By the next Thanksgiving, just to show off, my husband cooked the neck and innards in one of my own cooking pans.

"That's not going into my gravy," I informed him, waving my wooden spoon menacingly.

"No, no, it's for the dog," he said. "She'll love it."

He was right. The dog did. I haven't felt the same about the dog since.

I move that our Thanksgiving meals feature a dish that has never had a head or a neck or giblets.

Lasagne, anyone?

# BREAKING THE
# THANKSGIVING MOLD

When I first suggested to my family that we celebrate Thanksgiving away from home, all family members declined. Vigorously. But after years of serving the same Thanksgiving Day dinner to the same people at the same table, I vowed to blast my husband and two teenaged sons out of their annual November rut.

Guerilla tactics were required. I opened the battle on the culinary front by leaving around recipes for curried capon and braised pheasant, chestnut oyster stuffing, and pumpkin-kiwi puree. I threatened to substitute crushed rice cakes for the squishy white bread in the stuffing, citing health considerations.

They surrendered, but with one stipulation. We could spend Thanksgiving away from home but everything, and they did mean everything, had better be exactly the same.

The day before Thanksgiving we loaded up the car with twenty-five bags of groceries and provisions for our culinary orgy and headed toward the green, fog-brushed foothills of Inverness and our rented house.

We stop for dinner. The mood is somber and the meal punctuated by long silences, long looks at Mom and obvious disgust at every statement Mom makes. Unfortunately, the *Psychology Today* article, "Let's Stop Blaming Mom," won't come out until a year later.

Our 17-year-old drives the second lap of the trip. When

we hit a winding section of road, he keeps driving as if we're still on the freeway. All three of us begin wincing, sucking in our breath, and screaming at him to slow down and stay away from the edge of the road, where there is a steep drop off into oblivion. I wonder if we'll live to see Thanksgiving.

The road to the house, which leaves Sir Francis Drake Boulevard at a 90 degree, gravity-defying angle, appears suddenly.

"Turn left," barks my husband and, tires squealing, we do.

Our driver maintains his speed on the hairpin turns as his rapidly aging father tries to decipher the crumpled hand-drawn map while urging, "Slow down, damn it, slow down."

We thread our way to a spot that feels like the end of the earth. Only by prowling around on foot in the dark woods with flashlights do we locate the four-inch wooden sign which marks the descent to the house.

In silence, we follow the narrow path to the house. Inside, a cold blast of air hits us. The owner has warned me there is no central heating and we have come prepared with $100 worth of long underwear and supermarket fireplace logs, but it is colder than I imagined.

It begins to rain as we lug in the twenty-five bags of groceries, the suitcases, the sleeping bags, the firewood, and the hair dryers. Suddenly we notice a newt frozen on the path, trying to be invisible. A bag gives way and a carton of milk splats on the ground. The look on the newt's face is sheer terror. Our laughter breaks the silence and we are friends again.

Later, we sit in front of the fire and drink hot cider. The adventure of finding the house has been a bonding experience. Since there is no TV, my son turns on the record player and the music of Mozart fills the room. We do not ever sit at home like this. We're all too busy, always going somewhere else. It feels so good. I know this will be a Thanksgiving we'll never forget.

During the night a storm blows the trees and dashes rain against the roof and windows. It is soothing and restful and adds to the sense of adventure. Later my husband tells me it was the best sleep he'd had in months.

I wake up early, slip on my thermal bathrobe, and prepare to be Pioneer Earth Mother taming the wilds for her family.

I plug in the space heater and put water on the stove to boil. Warmth and hot chocolate will greet my family when they emerge from their dens. Outside, the wind makes the trees dance and smears the windows with rain.

I arrange my little jars of poultry seasoning and sage and hum quietly. I reach over to flip on a light. No light. I check the heater. No heat. Same with the stove.

Fortunately the phone works but I hesitate to use it, hoping to keep this potential disaster a secret.

It begins to rain harder. The leaves on the trees turn inside out and wind rattles the door.

I dial Pacific Gas and Electric. A recording tells me to call another number. I wait fifty rings before someone answers. I tell them the power is out in Inverness. A voice tells me the power is not out in Inverness. And what's our address? I don't know the address. All I know is a little wooden sign at the top of a hill.

I call the owner to find out the address. I call PG & E, wait the fifty rings again, and tell them the address. Once again, I'm informed there is no outage in Inverness.

"Besides, San Francisco and Mill Valley are out. When we get them back on line, we'll worry about you."

By then the teenagers are standing around my chair,

saying things like, "Does this mean we can't shave or blow dry our hair? What about the turkey dinner? Boy, this was your dumbest idea yet, *Mom*."

I am spared further abuse by the sound of footsteps on the porch. A friendly neighbor tells us two large trees have blown down the line that leads to our house and to our house only. Tree crews will have to come out first and chop down the trees. This will take about four hours. Then, and only then, can PG & E repair the wires.

"I hope you weren't planning on cooking a turkey today," he says kindly. I want to run away with him.

He suggests we try to get reservations for dinner at Jerry's Farm House and Sea Food Restaurant in Olema. Before my family can pack for home, I dial Jerry's. After a long pause and some paper rustling, a nice lady says to come at 2 o'clock.

We while away the hours nibbling on cold Danish and trying to boil water in the fireplace. Our unshowered, unshaven, unblow-dried sons refuse to speak to us. My husband and I go for a walk in the rain and end up arguing about how far to walk. When we come in the house, our sons get up and walk stiffly into the other room. Only the fact that it is a Major Holiday keeps me from yelling at them. Of course it doesn't help that underneath I feel guilty.

By the time we head for Olema, the tree crew has arrived and the sun is out. My husband and I are charmed by the green countryside, the stone fences, the tidy farmhouses with smoke curling out of the chimneys, and the fresh, crisp air.

From the back seat, I sense great rolling of the eyes.

We arrive at Jerry's at 2:00 sharp. The hostess tells us they've heard about us and wanted to offer us their ovens to cook our turkey. Unfortunately, their own needs made this impossible.

I try to look regretful that we hadn't been able to lug our twenty-five bags of groceries down to their ovens, but secretly I'm thrilled. I had accomplished the coup of a lifetime. Not only was I celebrating Thanksgiving away from home, I'd escaped cooking as well.

Dinner is wonderful. The turkey is succulent, the sweet potatoes delicious, the warm rolls exquisite. Sunlight streams in through the windows. A family with two adorable children and a baby eat at the table next to us.

Our teenaged critics find fault with everything. Too much onion in the stuffing, turkey too dry, gravy too thick and green besides. And they're grossed out by the baby who they claim drooled and rubbed sweet potatoes in her hair.

After pumpkin pie, we drive out to Point Reyes Lighthouse. My husband had hoped to see migrating whales, but a thick fog rolling in makes it difficult to even see the lighthouse. But we do see deer darting gracefully back and forth across the road, through the fog.

We return home at dusk. As we crest the hill, we see light streaming from our house. The PG & E crews are just leaving. We cheer and honk and wave.

After a light supper, we once again sit together in the same room. While the adults play Trivial Pursuit, one kid reads a Stephen King book, and the other one sketches. But I can tell they are present because every once in a while they say something like, "Hey Mom! Brazil is *not* a city."

Together two nights in a row. What a miracle. What a Thanksgiving.

Two days later we drive our turkey and our twenty-five bags of groceries back home and I serve the same Thanksgiving Day dinner to the same people at the same table.

And it is good.

# GRIEF OVER GRAVY

Gravy, the quiet brown menace that arrives on the table in its own boat is, without question, the root cause of most Thanksgiving Day hissy fits. And what will surely develop into a nationwide problem within three to five years, is already a crisis in California, the Golden State being on the leading edge of life, cuisine, and other problems.

Gravy is completely at odds with the California lifestyle. Maybe cooks make gravy regularly in Cleveland, but the brown stuff has virtually disappeared from the repertoire of the California cook. Gravy is nostalgia, along with deep dish apple pie, baking powder biscuits, and Spam.

We Californians prefer to occupy ourselves with salmon over mesquite or chicken with artichokes. Perhaps an occasional mustard caper reduction sauce, but gravy? Not in a pig's eye.

Would a true Californian (i.e. anyone living here more than 6 months) really want to fuse hot grease, white flour and water, or stand at a stove upwards of half an hour, stirring and scraping and straining, and then consume the end product? Let's face facts. It's just not our way. We've evolved to a higher plane.

Now this works fine except for the last Thursday in November. On that day, the entire nation executes an about-face and assumes a Midwestern tilt. Suddenly we believe that serving a plate of turkey, mashed potatoes, and stuffing devoid of a thick brown blanket of gravy is to violate a basic tenet of Western civilization.

Thus all cooks, regardless of age, race, or sexual preference are expected to produce gravy on Thanksgiving.

And not just mediocre stuff. No, the gravy standards in this country are high. It must be the correct color (brown); consistency (lump free); density (not too thick, not too thin) and flavor (superb). In fact the flavor must not suggest that any of the actual ingredients have been used in its preparation.

The problems here are obvious. First, the instructions for the preparation of gravy have disappeared. Gravy has been squeezed out of modern cookbooks by goat cheese and Greek meatballs. And few households have a resident Grandma who can impart the secrets of gravy. Besides, Grandma is probably a militant vegetarian who runs a pottery studio and does Rolfing in the back room.

Then there are the tricky, interpersonal problems. This complicated cooking maneuver, performed only once a year and right before a five-course meal, is rife with possibilities for hissy fits.

Not even having a firm grip on the process guarantees peace. My husband and I invariably "have words" because he claims I "take too long" making the gravy while the rest of the food gets cold.

That's probably because I learned to make gravy from my stepmother who came to cooking late in life. She prepared it every Sunday with an intensity that suggested brain surgery, probably because after each meal my father would assign her gravy a grade (usually a B plus or A minus). He always compared hers with the apex of his gravy experience—that served by the U.S. Army during World War II.

Another couple we know prepares Thanksgiving dinner together, with matching degrees of culinary zeal and ecstasy—until the gravy. Then with wooden spoons raised, they engage in their annual fight—do you put the giblets into the gravy whole or do you chop them up?

A friend came close to filing for divorce after she'd spent the entire day in the kitchen, alone, cooking for her husband's relatives while he tinkered and hid out in the garage and they gossiped about her in the living room.

After everyone was summoned to the table and the food brought in, my friend lifted the cover from the gravy boat. She was rewarded with a stunned silence.

Finally her husband blurted out, "Good God, woman! Your gravy is gray!"

She told me next year she's going to have a migraine on Thanksgiving; or run away from home which, by the way, is a popular fantasy for many women around this time of year.

Personally, I'm ready to ditch gravy. My arteries don't need it and it's not on my nutritional plan. Furthermore, my kids won't touch it. Not since one of them asked me, "What exactly is gravy anyway?" When I told him, he looked at me, appalled, and said, "You're kidding."

Then he narrowed his native Californian eyes and said, "Just who invented gravy anyway?

"I can just see it—a bunch of guys sitting around saying, 'Hey, let's just suppose we mix fat with flour and water and see what happens, ha ha.'"

I think he has the proper intellectual grasp of the situation.

Is gravy really a tradition worth saving?

I say it's time we jump ship and abandon the gravy boat.

A little kumquat yogurt sauce, anyone?

# THE ANNUAL FAMILY PHOTO

When the ironing board goes up and Mom encourages all family members to bring her their tired, their poor, their wrinkled clothing, the family knows it's the day The Picture will be taken.

Unless, of course, they've already intuited said event from the hastily scheduled haircut appointments of the previous week.

The annual picture-taking session has been a ritual in our house for ten years and it's the one day all four of us must look absolutely perfect, simultaneously, because this picture will be sent, enclosed in Christmas cards, all across the United States to relatives, high school chums, and college friends, all of whom I want to impress.

The early years were easier because I could choose the outfits my sons would wear, without any interference from the participants. But as our sons got older, the day became marred by conversations such as, "You're not going to wear that shirt, are you?" and "When is the last time you washed your hair?" and "No, you cannot wear your punk rock sunglasses in the picture."

The year my younger son hit sixteen he told me, "If you make me get a haircut before the picture, it'll be a Mohawk."

Once all four of us are more or less well-groomed, a feat accomplished only by my crabby and constant vigilance, we need someone to capture this moment on film.

Over the years, we've exhausted the small group of friends, both bosom and non, we've dared ask to snap our picture. Friends imposed upon in the past stop calling at this time of year, so irritated are they at having come over for what was billed as a half-hour session, only to spend half the day traipsing around our puny, suburban yard while we tried to find a place to be photographed where other people's houses, campers, boats, and garbage cans did not rise up in the background.

We finally found one good spot, but it required us to crouch down in front of some tall bushes. Unfortunately, the dog always arrived, sniffing us, trying to figure out what we were doing. All of these shots have my husband hissing, "Get the dog out of here," through clenched teeth, while doing a wan imitation of a smile.

We have tried including the dog, but her facial expression leaves something to be desired; she can't keep her drooling tongue in her mouth.

But no matter where the picture is taken, one of us (usually a child) refuses to smile, undoubtedly trying to get even with his parents for making him wear clean clothes. It's touches like these that give our family photographs all the ambiance of a Grant Wood painting.

One hardy picture-taking friend, who shot us two years in a row, brought her son along with his collection of goofy puppets to correct the smile problem. Alas, it didn't work. He cavorted with his puppets and made horns behind his mother's head while she focused the camera. We stared straight ahead muttering through rigid lips, "Stand up straight," "Don't fool with your hair," "What do you mean my lipstick is too dark," and "You're leaning on me, stupid."

"What are you guys, ventriloquists or something?" the son asked, throwing down his puppets in disgust.

The past few years we've been reduced to our own devices, like tripods and timers.

My husband lines us up tastefully against a wall, aims the camera, pushes a button, and rushes over to join us in a dead heat with the shutter. Unfortunately, he never quite makes it and his hurried presence in those pictures lends a certain rakish and unwelcome tilt to the proceedings.

One year he brought home a long, black tube with a squeeze bulb and promised he could arrange himself in the picture in a more orderly fashion with the black bulb in his hand and the other end attached to the camera.

There was one drawback. Although he tried holding the black bulb discreetly behind him, several relatives called to ask why he'd taken to carrying around a length of rubber hose.

This year we made new friends who actually volunteered, cheerfully, to come over and take our picture. They thought it sounded like "fun." Everything went smoothly. After ten years we are all eager to get it over with.

We all crouched down, plastered phony smiles on our faces and hissed, "Shoot, shoot already," to the startled photographer.

Once the picture taking session is over, the most difficult part is choosing a photograph where all four of us look reasonably intelligent and sane. But no matter which picture we (I) select, there is always one family member (usually a child) who swears it's the worst picture ever taken of him and he promises a boycott of next year's proceedings.

Oh well, I love these holiday rituals. They prevent me from plunging into that holiday depression one hears so much about.

For while I may act crazy and crabby, at least I'm not depressed.

So smile everybody, or live to regret it.

# LIBERATION FROM CHRISTMAS COOKIES

Liberation comes in small steps, often centered around seemingly innocuous events—trivialities to the casual observer. Yet deep within these events rest issues so profound, so full of meaning, that if the truth were known, the earth would have to stand still for a few moments to absorb the impact.

The issue I'm talking about is The Christmas Cookie.

The question is: whose job is it to roll the endless line of Christmas cookies down the ramps into Christmasdom? Whose job is it to fill that black hole into which Christmas cookies disappear?

For years, I carried the heavy sack of cookie expectations on my back. Gladly. More or less. Then suddenly there I was, balking at putting spoon to butter.

For a solid week I'd been waking up in the middle of the night worrying when I'd find time for baking. With a new job and the usual holiday pressures, time seemed very short.

Eventually I had to face the ugly truth: I no longer had any desire to bake Christmas cookies. Molasses, mincemeat, shortbread, roll out, cut out, press out, squish out—I wanted none of it. NONE of it, do you hear me?

The family was starting to get restless. At dinner one evening, both of my sons asked when I was going to start the cookies. After all, it was getting close to Christmas. I thought fast. I claimed I didn't have the ingredients. I considered telling them the stove was broken, but they'd see right through that.

In spite of my best efforts to resist, my female conditioning took over and I bought the ingredients for the two kinds of cookies we always make: Greek cookies called Kourabiedes and molasses cut-outs. The latter taste mediocre but are strong enough to hold three cups of colored frosting and piles of red and green sugars. One year my husband suggested we give them out as door stops.

But still, I stopped short of making any baking commitments.

One night at dinner my husband suddenly blurted out, "Who's going to help me make Greek cookies?"

The two teenagers enthusiastically agreed even though, or perhaps because, they had big tests in school the next day.

As one, the three of them turned toward me.

"Are you going to help?"

I looked vague and muttered something about Christmas cards.

I hung around the kitchen just a bit. It's always hard to let go.

"Find the recipe, will you?" my husband asked briskly, as he donned the apron that said "Kiss the Cook."

After I found the recipe, they flailed about, pulling out the Mixmaster, rooting around for the sherry and the flour. I stood back and watched. They didn't seem to notice me.

I slipped into the quiet living room and looked at the tree. I could hear them bickering mildly, so I put on some Christmas music.

Every once in a while I called in helpful hints like, "Don't make them too small, they dry out," and, "Close the drawers when you sift the flour."

Soon the cookies were in the oven. When they were done, they all trooped back to roll them into confectioner's sugar.

My oldest son came into the living room and popped one into my mouth. It was good. Very good.

How comforting to know that as I let go, others will be drawn into the kitchen to take up the cause. How wonderful to have it happening but not have to do it all.

Now that is liberation. And a true Christmas gift.

# CHRISTMAS TREE BLUES

Pity the poor Christmas tree. There it sits in the mountains, lost in lofty tree thoughts innocently manufacturing oxygen, when a bunch of bickering loudmouths runs up and chops it down. Or rather, saws it down, slowly and painfully with a dull and rusty blade.

Adding insult to injury, the sawing is preceded by disparaging remarks about the appearance of the tree, such as, "It has a bare spot a mile wide," or, "It looks like a Charlie Brown reject."

Then, the poor tree must listen to the fights about who is going to carry it down the hill, after which it is hustled into a compact car in a manner reminiscent of a mob kidnapping and driven out of the clean, crisp air of the mountains into the thick air of the valley, where it is promptly stuck into a contraption which features screws and metal things shoved cruelly into its trunk.

Every once in a while you'll get a tree that fights back. One year our tree, fully decorated of course, "fainted" twice. We had to secure it to the ceiling with hooks and picture wire. Several years ago another rebellious tree poked my husband in the eye, necessitating a trip to the emergency room, the wearing of an eye patch, and a lot of pain that lasted past New Year's.

Fortunately, most trees bear their burdens stoically, even enduring strangulation with electrical cords and scorching by lights. If the tree owners are merciful, they will have administered a drink of water and two aspirin. The truly merciful might administer something stronger, say a nice rum toddy.

Next, family members advance toward the tree carrying pretty shapes attached to pointy little hooks. I suspect most trees go unconscious at this juncture. By the time they come to, the tinsel, angel, and icicles are on, and perhaps the tree thinks it may have been worth it after all.

Now, people stand around and admire the tree; visitors exclaim about its beauty. Children keep it company reading Christmas stories and doing homework under it. Real little kids have been known to camp out under the tree in sleeping bags.

Pretty boxes tied with ribbons appear under its generous boughs. The sound of children giggling and whispering as they shake the boxes brings gladness to the heart of the evergreen.

By the time the family opens the gifts, accompanied by excited murmurs, shouts, and laughter, the tree is undoubtedly lulled into a false sense of security. It probably believes it will become a permanent part of the family and from now on, life will be glorious.

No such luck.

The next day, it hears things like, "Will you look at the mess in here? I can't stand it," and, "This tree is dropping needles like crazy."

By week's end, people are casting about for ways to "get rid of" the tree.

Children, at least, are sensitive to Christmas trees. I realized this when our son was about five. One day soon after Christmas, a group came to our door while my son was taking his nap. They offered to cart our tree away for fifty cents. Knowing a good deal when we heard it, we ripped off the decorations, flung them on the sofa, and handed our tree over to strangers.

When our son came downstairs from his nap, still in his nap costume (underwear), the first thing he said was, "What happened to the Christmas tree?" We pointed down the street to the car with a trailer on the back, now filled with anonymous Christmas trees, heading for a landfill.

He leaped out the front door and ran down the street, barefoot and still in his underwear, shouting, "You bring back my Christmas tree right now." I'm sure the tree, if it heard, appreciated the gesture. However, a futile gesture it was. He wasn't even allowed to cross the street to where the trailer sat. He returned home, defeated, and did the only thing he could—bawled his head off for half an hour until all the grief over the lost tree had worked its way out of his small body.

Now he is grown up and says things like the tree is "too small" or has a "bare spot" or is "weird looking." And even, "When are you going to take it down?"

Pity the poor Christmas tree. It gives us its all—beauty, fragrance, a home for the gifts. It holds up all the ornaments without complaint, from the fragile glass sphere handed down from Grandma to the ten-pound snowman made from bread dough and macaroni.

And what does it get in return? The tree will find itself outside, next to the garbage cans, bereft of any ornament save for a few strands of tinsel, without benefit of aspirin and water, waiting to be hauled away. This year we're instructed to cut our trees into four foot lengths so they may more easily be ground into compost. A grim end from such a noble beginning.

Before I take off the decorations and carry the tree outside, I'm going to whisper a few loving words to it and pat its drying needles. I just hope a little kindness can ease a broken heart.

# MOM
# GETS
# OUT

# PULSATING PURSES

Several years ago I became aware that my purse was separate from my body. For more years than I care to think about, I had considered it as simply another appendage.

My only explanation for this is that whenever I was out shopping, my children—two rowdy boys born eighteen months apart—had so consumed my attention, I hadn't had the mental reserves to realize that the pouch I was pawing and fumbling through was not permanently attached.

Now that they're in school and I can go out by myself, I've become painfully aware of how un-savoir-faire I look to grocery clerks and exasperated shoppers as I scramble and rifle through the contents of my satchel, trying to locate my checkbook.

There has been a standing joke in the family about how long it takes me to find anything. They claim it's quicker to break into the house or jump start the car than to wait for me to find my keys.

I've always imagined that if a burglar chased me home, he'd be able to kill me, very slowly, before I could find my keys and get into the house.

So anyway, when consciousness dawned, I noticed I was dragging around a purse with three compartments. I was forever scrambling back and forth through each nasty section looking for something or other. And whatever the item, it was crusted with a layer of ancient graham cracker crumbs, left over from episodes of shopping with small persons.

I resolved to stop torturing myself and bought a purse with one large compartment. My stuff might get jumbled up, but the chances of finding anything would always be 100 percent instead of 33⅓ percent, reasoned my keen mind.

Like so many things, this worked in theory but not in practice. While everything was in one place, it was now eight layers deep, and I was still pawing. Except now, I had to take everything out of the purse, layer by layer. Talk about undignified—crumpled Kleenex, the bright green comb the dog had chewed, the wallet, ink-stained from when the pen bled to death. The entire contents of my purse went on display every time I needed a pencil.

So, I reasoned, bigger would be better. I located a purse big enough to carry not only my usual collection but my lunch and a book as well. It worked great for awhile.

Then I noticed a few drawbacks.

First, since it was so large, people couldn't get around me in crowded places. They were forever pushing against my purse and rotating me along with it, making me dizzy.

The second drawback was my family. When they realized I had a tiny bit of extra room, they lined up to borrow a space. My husband handed me his wallet and sunglasses. My older son handed me his camera and extra film. And the younger son once asked if I could carry home a half-eaten hamburger he wanted to save for the dog.

Like most women, I am burdened with the desire to please everyone, so I accepted these donations. But I resented it.

My purse became so heavy, I felt tired the minute I stood up.

Then I read that doctors claimed women who carried

heavy purses developed uneven shoulders and deformed their spines.

Not wanting to become a cripple, I went out and bought a small purse, a clutch. If I have less room, I'll carry less, right?

Wrong. I could not part with a single thing. I need everything, including the Swiss Army knife, four pink lipsticks, fifteen broken pencils, sunglasses, wallet, checkbook, mirror, little box of aspirin, notebook, and keys.

I don't know what the answer is. I'm too old for a backpack and I'll never squeeze into a clutch. I could carry a briefcase, but I'd feel like an imposter. I could throw it all into a grocery bag and push it around in a shopping cart, like a bag lady. But I can just hear it now. "Hey Mom! Can you carry my bicycle?"

A few years ago I saw an Andy Rooney segment on "60 Minutes." He showed a film clip of us women dragging our purses around. Some of them were the size of suitcases. He claimed it was our purses that were holding us back from true liberation.

I believe it.

What I really need is someone else to carry my belongings for me—like a small monkey.

Or a wife.

# HIGH TECH MAKE-UP

I found myself at a make-up counter the other day. My little jar of blusher, purchased ten years ago, was almost empty and I needed a new supply.

I quickly selected Prairie Pink blusher, grabbed a matching lipstick and handed my purchases to a saleslady who wore so much make-up it looked like Boy George was her beauty consultant.

"How about some matching eye make-up?" asked the painted lady.

She snapped open a little box with three squares of color—tan, gray and pink.

"Pink eye lids? Are you kidding? I'd feel like Miss Piggy."

The clerk retaliated. She marched from behind the counter, pushed me backwards toward a stool, and ripped off my glasses.

"Sit," she commanded. "I'll do your eyes."

Then she stared long and hard.

"Are you using eye cream?" she demanded.

"Uh, no," I confessed.

"You should. Your lids are dry," she said with authority.

She whipped out her arsenal of tubes, brushes, and sticks.

"First we put on highlighter, all the way up into your brows," she said, swatting at my eyes with a brush big enough to sweep out the garage.

"You don't have much space between your eyes and eyebrows," she informed me. I felt at a loss for words. "I'm sorry," didn't seem quite right.

Then she brushed gray powder from my eyes out to my temples.

I peered into the mirror. I looked like Dracula in drag.

"Don't worry. I'm going to lighten it out," she said, coming at me with a three-foot long Q-Tip.

She picked up speed. Some pink, then orange, then green. I imagined she was painting a full color sunset on each lid.

"Have you ever considered art school?" I asked. She ignored me.

"You do use eyeliner, don't you?" she asked.

It was my turn to ignore her. How could I admit to this hussy that my make-up routine is limited to slapping on foundation at home and putting on lipstick in the car? And as for eyeliner—I'd never forget the horrible experiences in the eighth grade girls' bathroom, trying to draw an even line on an eyelid with pencils sharpened with razor blades. No thank you; I'd rather keep my vision if she didn't mind.

Before I could leap out of the chair, she was at my eyelids again. But there was no sharp point, only a lovely, soft, crayony implement.

"Say, when did they invent those?" I asked.

She put down her equipment and looked at me with pity.

"My, my, you don't get out very much, do you?" she said.

"You do use mascara, don't you?" she asked, going for the jugular. "No!" I almost shouted. "My lashes are very dark. I didn't think I needed it."

"Mascara separates and curls them," she informed me, in a tone that suggested I was an imbecile.

I backed down while she applied what felt like a layer of glue to my lashes.

Suddenly my poor little unsophisticated eyes started to tear.

"Oh dear, I've made you cry," she said, unsympathetically.

She handed me a tissue. "Just dab at the corners," she ordered.

The gunk was starting to ooze down my face. I imagined my face would soon look like a cow with muddy feet had run over it.

The clerk kept going. She covered my cheeks with pink blusher and pulled out her lipstick pencil. "You must define your edges," she said.

I grabbed my glasses and looked in the mirror. A refugee from vaudeville stared back at me.

"Look in a full-length mirror," she said. "That way you won't only see 'The Face.'"

I bolted from the store into broad daylight. Two little old ladies clutched their purses to their bosoms as I passed. Mothers pulled their children close. Others looked at my clothes as if to ask, "So where's the rest of the clown outfit?"

I finally made it to my front door. My son took one look at me and said, "Mom. What did you do? I'm not saying I don't like it but you look . . . well . . . older. Real old."

The other came to see what the fuss was about.

"Well, you certainly don't look like a mother," he noted.

I looked in the mirror. "How could I have let her do this to me?" I wailed. "I look like a fool."

"You're gullible? You couldn't see what she was doing?" they suggested.

"Wash it off," they pleaded, saying they had homework and couldn't afford to be distracted by my wails of anguish.

"Oh well. I guess I can stand it until your father comes

home," I told them. "Maybe he needs a good laugh." I promised to cut down on the moaning.

I endured a heavy, painted feeling until six o'clock. But the strangest part of the whole experience occurred when my husband came home. He wasn't at all startled by my face and didn't seem to notice anything was different. When I finally pressed him, he said he sensed there was something different about me, but he couldn't figure out exactly what.

Now that's scary.

# MOM'S TEDDY BEAR

It was one of those days. Inundated with furnace repair people, a sick husband, two teenage boys off from school, gritty floors to be vacuumed, meals to be made, and articles to be written, I decided to run away from home.

I drove to Los Altos, a nearby town with a real Main Street. I parked and browsed in the cute little shops, drifting into whichever took my fancy—a book store, a bakery, a gift shop.

It was in the gift shop that I found Edward.

He was sitting in an antique high chair with a lace bow tied rakishly around his neck.

I looked at him and he looked at me. I cocked my head to get a better look. He did the same.

Before I got too involved, I checked the price tag. No sense going ga ga over a $200 bear. The tag said $25.

I picked him up. He felt just right, like I imagined a pliable cat might feel.

This could be my surrogate cat, I decided. I'd been longing for a cat. I believed that I had to have one if I was ever to be a real writer. But my husband's allergies prevented it.

"Do you want a cat, or do you want me to be able to breathe in my own home?" was the way he put it.

While Edward could never purr at my feet, he could sit on the shelf over my typewriter and function in some editorial capacity. I could talk over ideas with him, or he could tell me, "No, you've gone overboard on that point," or "Leave that part out." Heaven knows I could use the help.

I walked around the store looking at other treasures: the plates with ducks and roosters and the mugs with clever sayings, but my heart belonged with Edward.

I returned. He winked at me. I picked him up and, holding him like a baby, took him to the cash register.

"Am I out of my mind?" I asked myself. A 39-year-old buying a teddy bear?

I handed Edward to the clerk. But no, wait. I took him back. Was he the very best bear? I checked out the row of other teddies. Some were short and fat, others fluffy and small. But clearly, Edward was the best bear in the store—a large bear with semi-fluffy fur, long arms and legs, a cute velveteen nose, and a round head cocked slightly to the side. He was a literary sort of bear. He would do me good.

I paid and took Edward home to meet the family.

My husband, who still has his original teddy from childhood, a tired looking bear named Sleepy, with the fur worn off and one eye missing, liked him immediately.

Then I introduced Edward to my two sons.

"Hey, let us play with him," they said, taking turns flipping his arms up and down. "Hey, he's loose," they observed.

Explaining that Edward was tired from his trip, I took him upstairs and tucked him in bed. That night he slept with my husband and me and I'm pleased to report Edward doesn't snore.

The next morning at breakfast, my 14-year-old asked, "Where's Edward? Is he sleeping in?"

"Er, yes."

"Can we go up and bring him down?"

"Uh, no," I said, stalling for time. What kind of mother wouldn't let her own sons play with her teddy bear? But I felt reluctant.

"He's uh, meditating," I said.

"I hope he doesn't belong to some weird, religious cult," my son said. "There's a lot of that going around."

"Oh, no, nothing like that. Edward's a Gestalt bear— very together, if you know what I mean."

"You mean he's an uptight bear?" they laughed.

"No, just well put together. Tight seams and all."

Fortunately they lost interest and left Edward to sit peacefully on my shelf. If his presence has improved my writing, it's hard to tell. His capacity for editorial guidance is not high, and if he has any opinions, he keeps them to himself. I guess he helps me the most when I pick him up and bury my face in his soft neck.

Every once in a while he catapults himself off his shelf onto my typewriter. I suspect he's trying to tell me what I'm writing is either very good or very bad.

Or maybe he's nearsighted and just trying to get a closer look. Hmm, I wonder how Edward would look in hornrims?

If I told you I bought him some clothes—a toddler T-shirt and overalls at a garage sale—would you think I was losing my mind?

I hope not, because that is exactly what I did. I couldn't stand to see him chilly and naked up there on the shelf.

After I'd had Edward for a few months, something amazing happened. After almost two decades of refusing, my husband decided he could live with a cat after all.

We found Agatha Christie hurt and crying in some bushes. We brought her home, nursed her back to health, and she decided to stay.

So now I have two soft furry things to bury my face in when the going gets tough. I can't say all this comfort has improved my writing, but it sure makes it more fun.

And muffles my cries.

# THE MUD BATH

Calistoga, Ca. "Take your clothes off and step into the mud," said the young woman.

My husband tore off his clothes and, propelled by embarrassment, quickly lowered himself into the sludge.

I, however, hesitated. Of the two discomforts—being naked in front of a stranger or inserting my body into what looked like the by-product of a dairy farm—I chose nakedness. Easily.

I had pictured a pristine tub filled with light brown clay, like the kind that comes in little jars of clay masque for facials.

Instead, I was faced with a cement bunker filled with smelly, furry-looking gunk. Furthermore, everything from floor to ceiling in the cinder block-lined room was encrusted with grit.

"Where does the mud come from?" I asked, stalling for time.

I prayed for an answer like, "Clear Springs Reservoir."

"It's a mixture of mud, volcanic ash, and peat moss," was the disappointing reply.

As I inched my toe toward the brown concoction, I tried to remember why I was there. Oh yes. The brochure said mud baths cleanse toxins from the body.

But that mud had been there awhile. How many other people's toxins were lurking in the peat moss? And what would prevent them from seeping into my body? Could I end up with extra?

I looked at my husband. Firmly embedded in the stuff, he looked like a creature in the movie, *Mud Man Lurks in Swamp.*

"Just get in," said the attendant sharply. "We're on a time schedule."

"Do other people have trouble getting in?" I asked.

"Yes," she hissed, coming closer.

Cursing the person who had recommended this activity, I fixed my eyes onto the ceiling and pushed my legs into the ooze.

The stuff was so thick it pushed my toes apart. I had to give it credit: the stuff had resistance. Maybe it didn't want me in there either.

Once I was "in," the attendant left the room. We were alone.

"Isn't this disgusting?" I asked my husband.

"Shh. I'm meditating," he said.

I tried to meditate too. I tried to imagine myself in a clean place far, far away. I tried to will my body to resist foreign toxins.

But the only pictures I could tune in were pigs. Little naked pink pigs rolling around in the barnyard.

Fifteen long minutes crawled by. Our warden returned. We were to get out of the mud, shower off, and climb into our Herbal Bath: two rickety bathtubs filled with tan water that smelled like medicated mouthwash.

Once again we were alone. Gazing at the cinder block walls, I imagined I was in a prisoner of war camp. I wondered if other inmates had put up fights before being wrestled into the mud.

I tried to talk to my husband but he told me he was "trying to relax."

After twenty minutes we were rescued and told to wrap up in towels. Next stop—the Herbal Blanket Wrap.

We were taken to a small room with two low beds. Mystical music played on a tape deck. Mystical paintings hung on the walls. I tried to feel mystical.

"Lie down," came the order.

First a sheet, then blankets, and more blankets were wrapped around us. Cold compresses were applied to our foreheads.

We were alone once again.

For awhile I continued with my usual obsessions—had my children been run over by cars or had the house burned down in my absence? But gradually the warmth and music pierced my awareness. I decided to let go and relax. My partner was probably on another planet by now, so I might as well get spacey too.

It worked. I imagined myself floating up over the earth. A golden light shone on me. I was floating. I was free...

"Psst," came a noise from the next bed. I tried to block it out.

"Psst." More insistent.

"WHAT IS IT?"

"Do you think we're supposed to tip?"

If I could have moved my arms, I'd have smacked him with a cold compress. But it was too late. The spell was broken. Every muscle went on red alert.

The tipping question plagued me during the final stage of treatment which featured a half-hour massage by a woman with strong hands and an accent. I never figured out the answer. Later, over Calistoga water at a nearby restaurant, my husband told me there had been a metal tray in his massage room and he'd tipped enough for both of us.

That problem solved, I tried to figure out how I felt.

The brochure said the treatment was a "natural" one that would help me "let go of habitual patterns."

All I knew was I felt limp.

Before our mud experience, we'd agreed to stop at antique stores along the way home.

But as we passed one shop after another, I didn't have the energy to get out of the car, let alone paw the goods.

Now that's breaking a habitual pattern.

I just hope it's not permanent.

I probably picked up somebody else's toxins. Somebody who hates antique shops.

Maybe I got my husband's.

# ADDENDUM

# THE EMPTY NEST

Each autumn, as new groups of unsuspecting parents fall into the empty nest, shock waves ripple through the ranks of the middle-aged. New victims seek each other out to ask if they've heard from their offspring and to whisper lamentations like, "I feel as if my life is over," and "Nothing will ever be the same."

This empty nest hits mothers and fathers with particular cruelty because, as with all parental experiences, we are unprepared for the intense feelings that suddenly surface. The grief is especially confusing for people like me who once longed for this day. Now that it's here, I wish it were not.

In some ways, it's like the end of a great love affair—after years of loving your children and living with them, you no longer share their lives. You don't hear about their daily highs and lows, share their jokes and humor, or get to pick up after them. They now live somewhere else. Their physical presence has been reduced to the possessions they left behind and an entry in your address book.

But, like everything else, the empty nest can be a mixed blessing. With the grief and sadness come a few bits of joy. There is, as they say, the bad news and the good news.

The pain begins building months before your son's or daughter's departure as you torture yourself with, "This is the last year, month, week, day, breakfast, lunch, dinner, time we watch 'Cheers' together," etc., and peaks as you watch your child turn away and walk into the dorm or onto the airplane or wherever it is his or her new life will begin.

Before, during, and after this peak experience you will find yourself in tears at odd moments. Anything can trigger the wet stuff: the sight of a dirty sneaker under a bed, a trumpet case left behind, a twisted toothpaste case as only your child could do it, or a forlorn container of Frusen Gladje ice cream in the freezer. Of course you may also cry when you realize that now you have to mow the lawn.

You immediately age twenty-five years as you turn into your parents—begging for phone calls, letters, visits, scraps of attention. You sit dejectedly by the phone, waiting, desperate to hear your child's voice. And when the call does come, you're lucky if your offspring grants you full attention. More likely, after every other sentence, he or she will holler down the hall to some unseen rival, "I'll be right there! As soon as I get off the phone!"

The grocery store becomes a vale of tears when you realize you have no one for whom to buy silly treats like Cracker Jacks. Worse still, it's depressing to realize you no longer live with anyone who bothers to unwrap the prize.

For some reason, many of your failures as a parent come up to haunt you. You find yourself remembering all the times when you didn't listen, when you blew up, when you called one of your children an "idiot." You hurt and wonder what was so important that you tromped all over them instead of respecting them for the special people they are. You wish you could do it all over again, and know this time you would be a much, much better parent.

You always come home to an empty house—no notes, no backpacks flung on the sofa, no footprints in the carpet you vacuumed three days ago.

You catch yourself doing strange things like talking baby-talk to the dog, or sitting in your child's empty room feeling lonely and wishing that at three o'clock he or she would come banging in the front door and holler "I'm home."

But after the dust settles and the intervals between tears increase, you begin to notice that there are some good parts to this experience.

For one thing, the kid's bed is made and the room is neat.

As you are no longer faced daily with their imperfections (as you see them), you no longer feel compelled to "fix" them by giving advice, lectures, and sermons. You feel, for the first time since they've been born, officially "off duty." It feels wonderful. You feel young again.

You notice your own moods and emotions. No longer is your attention riveted on the ups and downs of an adolescent in turmoil. You discover thoughts and feelings separate from them. It's exciting. Exhilarating.

You no longer hear, "What's for dinner?" the minute you open your eyes in the morning. You also no longer feel compelled to make dinner, complete with green and yellow vegetables, every night. You can eat donuts for dinner, if you want to.

No one from the PTA hounds you to attend meetings and serve on committees.

You and your husband, if the two of you survived and are still speaking, will have lots to talk about as you reminisce about every trip and experience you ever had with your children, remembering, of course, only the good parts.

No neighbors come over to complain your children have thrown dog poop over the fence onto the side of their house. Toilet-paperings of your own house fall off dramatically.

You feel free to loaf on Sundays instead of thinking you should organize yardwork parties to set a good example or just to squeeze some work out of your children.

You no longer feel compelled to stay home for the

kids—even though the kids stopped staying home for you years ago!

You can find a pen, a pencil, the glue, the scissors. Drinking glasses are now in the kitchen cupboard instead of spread out all over the house.

You get sole access to the VCR. No one tapes over your TV programs or seethes at you for taping over theirs.

You can do sappy things like get out slides and look at their baby pictures and sob as you see them small again and remember how they felt and smelled when you held them in your arms.

And you notice how young you looked back then. You realize a big part of your life is over. And you wonder which makes you sadder—their leaving or your growing older.

Fortunately, you now have the time for doing what those pictures inspire you to do—go to exercise class, start a diet, and look into liposuction surgery.

These activities help to take your mind off your slightly broken heart, which is working hard to mend itself as it waits for a letter or phone call, some word from your loved ones, and reassurance that even though they have their own lives now apart from you, they haven't forgotten you.

A final observation: although you now feel as if you don't have children, a letter or phone call can quickly activate those dormant parental hormones and turn you into a mass of turmoil and emotion—just like when they were living at home.

So maybe it's never really over.

I'm not sure if that's the bad news or the good news.

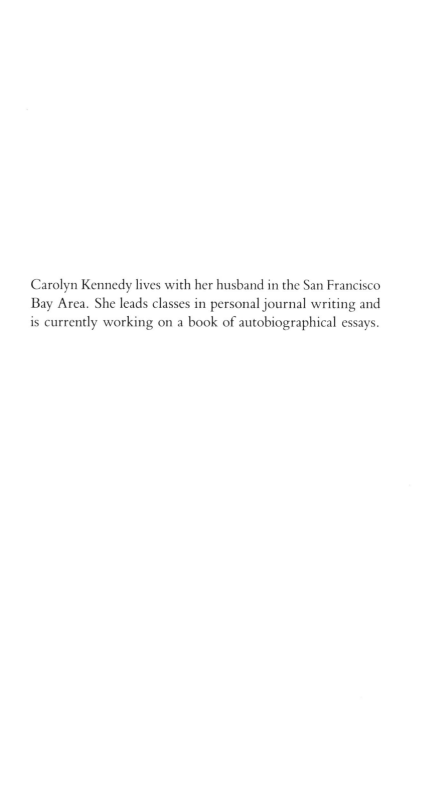

Carolyn Kennedy lives with her husband in the San Francisco Bay Area. She leads classes in personal journal writing and is currently working on a book of autobiographical essays.

*Ordering By Mail*

To order a copy of *Bulletins from the Home Front,* send your name, address and a check or money order for $7.00 plus $2.00 for postage and handling to:

CHERRY TREE PRESS
P.O. Box 73
Palo Alto, CA 94301

California residents please add $.58 tax.

If you are ordering more than one book, include an additional $.50 each for postage and handling.